Beat Procrastination

AND

Make the Grade

The Six Styles of Procrastination and
How Students Can Overcome Them

DR. LINDA SAPADIN

WITH JACK MAGUIRE

PENG

PENGUIN BOOKS

Published by the Penguin Group
Penguin Putnam Inc., 375 Hudson Street,
New York, New York 10014, U.S.A.
Penguin Books Ltd, 27 Wrights Lane,
London W8 5TZ, England
Penguin Books Australia Ltd, Ringwood,
Victoria, Australia
Penguin Books Canada Ltd, 10 Alcorn Avenue,
Toronto, Ontario, Canada M4V 3B2
Penguin Books (N.Z.) Ltd, 182–190 Wairau Road,
Auckland 10, New Zealand

Penguin Books Ltd, Registered Offices:
Harmondsworth, Middlesex, England

First published in Penguin Books 1999

10 9 8 7 6 5 4 3 2 1

LIBRARY OF CONGRESS CATALOGING IN PUBLICATION DATA
Sapadin, Linda.
    Beat procrastination and make the grade: the six styles of procrastina-
tion and how students can overcome them / Linda Sapadin with Jack
Maguire.
      p. cm.
    ISBN 0 14 02.7801 X
    1. Study skills.   2. Procrastination.   3. Students—Time management.
I. Maguire, Jack, 1945– . II. Title.
LB1049.S412   1999
378.1'70281—dc21   99–18017

Printed in the United States of America
Set in Sabon
Designed by Jessica Shatan
Illustrations by Stan Shaw

To
my husband Ron
and my sons
Brian, Glenn, and Daniel
who have inspired me to be the best I can be

Acknowledgments

Writing a book is a long, frustrating process in which it helps to be nurtured and encouraged by the people who believe in you. I have been blessed to have many such supportive people in my life and it is my pleasure to acknowledge their contribution.

My greatest thanks and appreciation to my husband, Ron Goodrich. He is a loving human being as well as a gifted and creative psychologist. Whenever I am confused or stuck on some issue, he is always ready to provide an insightful idea or perspective to help me move beyond my impasse. Ron, I want you to know how much I appreciate your calm reassurance, your optimism, and your love for me. No problem seems so difficult or complex when you are there to listen.

One of the greatest joys of my life is being a mom to three of the most interesting and beautiful people I know. My sons, Brian, Glenn, and Daniel, each in his unique way, have been my number one power source.

Brian, your enthusiasm for life, your appreciation of music, and your willingness to "go for it," even when it's not the conventional way, are a constant source of inspiration for me.

Glenn, your imaginative spirit and social, friendly personality are a delight to me and your outrageous sense of humor always keeps me smiling.

Danny, your self-confidence, sensitivity, and sensibility

are a magical combination that I greatly admire, respect, and learn from.

Being a part of your interesting lives, my sons, from the beginning to this very moment, has been my privilege.

My loving appreciation to my sister, Ruth Grant, and my brother, Bob Fink. We have been through much together in this journey of life. It's always great to celebrate the joys and triumphs with you!

This is the second book I've completed with an extraordinary team of supportive people.

To Jack Maguire, my co-writer, my deepest graditude. We worked well together to make it happen. I thank you for your hard work, insight, patience, and good humor.

To Jane von Mehren, my editor and publisher at Penguin, many thanks for your honest feedback and sincere desire to make this book the best it could be. Your editorial suggestions given in a clear, gentle, and helpful manner are much appreciated.

To Faith Hamlin, my agent, thanks for believing in me from the very beginning. I am grateful for your confidence, trust, and faith in me as a writer, so much so that I have grown to own them myself.

To Jennifer Ehmann, new to the team, thanks for your enthusiasm and editorial input which helped improve the flow and clarity of the final manuscript.

Finally, thanks to the students who willingly shared their stories with me and to my clients who agreed to let their work with me be of help to you. Respecting your confidentiality, I have altered identifying information by creating composite characters for many of the stories in this book.

Contents

1

Mastering the Student Experience

Being a student can be the time of your life, during which you enjoy new freedoms, friends, and experiences. However, if you have a procrastination problem, your college dreams may seem more like nightmares.

You've got classes to attend, papers to write, tests to study for, teaching styles to figure out, and an academic future to plan. You also have to manage your personal affairs, maintain good relationships with family members and friends, and, possibly, work to earn money. Then there are all the things you need to do to keep yourself healthy, sane, and motivated, like getting enough sleep, exercise, and recreation; managing sudden crises; and taking advantage of interesting social and cultural opportunities.

All of these demands on your time are difficult enough to balance under the best conditions. When you routinely procrastinate on even just a few of them, they can soon overwhelm you. Let's consider two brief examples.

Carly, a freshman at a liberal-arts college and a part-time veterinary assistant, was crushed when she finally had to drop out of one course and apply for incompletes in two others because she couldn't keep up with the assignments. Forced to take a semester's leave of absence to catch up, she came to me feeling frazzled and scared, complaining, "I can't believe this is happening! I've always been a good student and a hard worker. But over the past couple of years, despite my best efforts, I keep winding up with more than I can handle. And it's not my fault. People expect too much of me. My teachers, my boss, my parents—they're all so demanding. How am I supposed to please each and every one of them, and have any sort of social life, let alone time to myself?"

Tim, another client of mine, was a graduate student in business who seemed to have an entirely different problem. He was suffering serious doubts about whether he was cut out to get his MBA. He sounded less desperate than Carly, but equally caught in a bind. "Sometimes it drives me and others in my life absolutely crazy," he admitted, "but I just can't get motivated to study or do research until the last possible moment, when my back's against the wall. Up to that point, I'll do anything except what I know I have to do. I'll spend hours and hours reading stuff that's not really important. I'll go the gym, or hang with friends, or surf the 'net, or space out watching TV. But you know, I don't enjoy any of these things the way I should because of all the stuff hanging over my head. It's like I'm powerless to change. I've been this way for as long as I can remember. So far I've always come through in the end. Now, I'm not so sure I will—the stakes are much higher. I guess only time will tell!"

Although Carly and Tim differed greatly in the specific ways they created problems for themselves, they had one major thing in common that lay at the heart of their difficulties: They were both chronic procrastinators.

Every student procrastinates occasionally. A math whiz

who usually completes her homework on time may delay a required reading of *Moby-Dick* because the last thing she wants to do is plunge into a seafaring novel. A lit major may choose to read *Moby-Dick* for hours even if it's not required merely to avoid cleaning up after an especially rowdy party.

For many students, however, the problem of procrastination is much more pervasive and deeply rooted. Because they learned as children to think, speak, and behave in specific ways, they have an inclination to procrastinate—and usually do—whenever they face a demanding situation. As they advance through high school, college, and graduate school, the predisposition typically grows much more troublesome, as classroom and lifestyle pressures become increasingly complex and weighty. At any point along this academic journey, their procrastinating ways can jeopardize, postpone, or even destroy their plans, hopes, and futures.

College-bound highschoolers often experience their first disturbing procrastination problem when it comes time for them to fill out college applications, take their SATs, and think seriously about what the college experience is going to be like. Here's how Rebecca, a sixteen-year-old junior in high school, feels at precisely this time in her life:

Frankly, I'm more scared than excited about going to college. Everything seems so overpowering. I've got a big cardboard box in my room that's stuffed to the max with admissions forms, SAT forms, ACT forms, college guidebooks, and magazine articles about college life. I look at that box and say, "I can't deal with this yet!" But my dad keeps saying I have to start working on it right away, or I'll be sorry later on. As a junior, I still think it's too soon. I'm too busy just trying to keep up my grades. I'd like to be able to do everything in one day, but I know it won't all get finished that way, so I don't even start.

And that's not all. I worry about the heavy workload once I finally get to college. How will I ever handle it, and do all the other stuff I have to do on my own? No one's going to be there like my parents making sure I get up on time, do all my homework, have clean clothes to wear, and meals on the table.

Sometimes, a long-term tendency to procrastinate doesn't really strike a student as a critical problem until the other end of the academic spectrum—graduate school. Usually this happens because graduate students are handling more responsibilities than ever before and playing for greater stakes: more advanced knowledge, more sophisticated skills, a better job, more money. Read what Danny, a part-time graduate student with a full-time job, has to say:

It's a much bigger strain than I thought, going to graduate school and working full-time. I can't seem to figure out when to do my assignments or, rather, how to do them in the time I've got available. Sometimes I find I procrastinate simply because there's so much to do and I don't know where to begin.

I don't like feeling that I have to cut back to three or four hours of sleep a night, although often that seems to be my only choice. Sometimes I just figure, "What the heck—I deserve a life, too," and I refuse to crack open a book even when I do have the time to study and know I have to do it."

In recent years the tendency to procrastinate has become even stronger among students, thanks to greater, more stressful competition for grades, status, jobs, and career prospects. According to a UCLA study tracking 75,000 college attendees over a twenty-year period, scarcely 40 percent of today's students actually complete requirements for their bachelor's degrees in four years as they originally intended to do, compared to over 47 percent twenty years ago. Alexander Astin, the principal author of this study, states that the main reasons why students do not complete their degree requirements as planned despite their serious efforts is because they fail to assess priorities, finish projects, and handle distractions. All of these factors are key elements of procrastination.

Fortunately, you can rid yourself of your tendencies to procrastinate. This book tells you how to do it, no matter what stage of the student experience you are now going through. If you're a highschooler, you can nip this problem in the bud so that your college years will be much more satisfying and productive than they otherwise would have been. If you're tackling this problem in, say, your sophomore year of college, you'll be far better off as a junior. If you're finally dealing with it in graduate school, your degree and your life afterward will be much more pleasant and enjoyable.

First thing to do if you want to beat procrastination is to recognize how you personally go about procrastinating. You'll learn the six basic styles later in this chapter and take quizzes to identify which ones cause you the most difficulty. Second comes a closer examination of each individual style, revealing how its particular bad habits develop, and, most important, what specific steps you can take to replace those bad habits with more effective ones.

Right now let's gauge your overall tendency to procrastinate. How serious is it? To get a better idea, ask yourself each of the following questions, circling "YES" if you *often* do what's described, and "NO" if you *rarely* or *never* do it:

- Do I plan study times with friends that turn into bull sessions about "important" things, like the best microbrew in town? **YES NO**

- Do I feel skilled at discussing symbolism in contemporary works, like *Star Wars* movies, but seem unable to discuss symbolism in classic works, like Shakespeare's plays? **YES NO**

- Do I leave a whole group of assignments unfinished for a long period of time, jumping from one to another without actually completing any? **YES NO**

- Do I wait until the last minute before starting to study for an exam? **YES NO**

- Do I flip out before an exam, getting angry with myself for not studying more ahead of time? **YES NO**

- Do I think I'm somehow special, and don't need to do all the things that other students need to do? **YES NO**

- Do I avoid assignments I think are boring, even if I know not doing them will affect me adversely? **YES NO**

- Do I ask, entice, cajole, beg, or bribe other people to do work I know I should do myself? **YES NO**

• Do other things, like organizing my CDs or listening to my roommate's problems, become more compelling to me when I have to study or finish an assignment?   YES   NO

• Do I put off doing an assignment until I can find the best time to do it, or until the best time presents itself?   YES   NO

• Do I take a break from studying to watch one TV program, but wind up staying tuned to the set for hours?   YES   NO

• Do I find myself thinking there's no time like tomorrow to do whatever needs to be done today?   YES   NO

• Do I feel I have lots of time to do a project when it's first assigned, then later feel I didn't have enough time to do it?   YES   NO

• Do I give stock responses to justify why I don't take action on projects, like "I work best under pressure," "I didn't have time," or "I just can't get inspired?"   YES   NO

• Do I find that I consistently wait until later to work on a project, creating lots of stress for myself—especially right before the deadline?   YES   NO

• Do I tell myself, "I've got to change the way I do things," but somehow never make any change?   YES   NO

• Do I find that a quick break, like a trip   YES   NO
to the mall, takes all afternoon, or a
group study session turns into a whole
night of just hanging with friends?

• Do I think that much of the time I   YES   NO
spend online is a way to avoid doing
what I need to do?

If you circled "YES" in response to *any* of these questions, you have a procrastination problem. The more "YES" answers you gave, the more serious your problem is. Whatever your total may be, don't despair about it or go to the other extreme and brush it off. Reading this book, taking the quizzes, and doing the self-help exercises that it provides will show you a better way to cope with all the life challenges you face now and in the future.

Chronic Procrastinators: An Overview

As individuals, chronic procrastinators have their own idiosyncratic methods of procrastinating; but as a group, they share certain distinctive traits and experiences. Above all, they're filled with good intentions about doing things, yet they can't seem to avoid putting them off. They're also inclined to rationalize or excuse their behavior on the grounds that it's nothing they can—or should—do anything about. They'll say to themselves things like, "I'm just lazy by nature," or they'll make claims to others such as, "I can't sit down and get myself to focus on a paper unless I have two or three days with nothing else to do." It's as if their tendency to procrastinate were a fact of life as unalterable as having brown eyes or being allergic to milk, rather than an acquired habit that they are, in fact, fully capable of changing.

Many times, students who chronically procrastinate seem very cool about it. They deflect or prevent outside criticism by making a joke of it. "You know how I am," they may laugh to their bewildered roommate as they finally get around to tackling an important assignment. "I put everything off as long as I can!" They may even boast about it, secretly feeling superior to others who are more time conscious: "I didn't even begin this term paper until late Friday night, and I still got it done by Monday morning's deadline!"

Actually this kind of self-justification, so typical of chronic procrastinators, is a form of self-deception. Instead of taking a good look at their problem and learning how to overcome it, they gloss over it. In doing so, they ignore the trouble it brings them, the difficulties it creates for others, and their personal need to deal with it—not only to get tasks done, but also to become stronger, happier, and more self-confident individuals.

The period from high school through, possibly, graduate school is the time when you are making the awesome, across-the-board transition from being a dependent adolescent to becoming an independent adult. You are struggling on *every* front with brand-new responsibilities to manage your own time, energy, and resources. Meanwhile, your most pressing obligation is getting a good education and, in the words of Stephen Covey, author of the recent bestseller *The 7 Habits of Highly Effective People*, "The main thing is to keep the main thing the main thing."

What, specifically, are the most significant tasks involved in this "main thing" (getting a good education)? It helps to sort them out so that none of them gets overlooked, undervalued, or shortchanged:

• Attending Classes

This means much more than simply sitting through a class, or putting in your time. It's a matter of really *being there*. It's keeping yourself alert, rather than fighting off fatigue from last night's bar-hopping, giving into daydreams of what you'll be doing next summer, or nursing a negative attitude toward the subject at hand. It's listening carefully to what others are saying, instead of just hearing their words. It's taking good notes, rather than merely copying what's on the board or hastily jotting down assignments. It's asking relevant questions, rather than remaining silent and uninvolved. You need to help yourself *use* valuable class time as well as you can, instead of simply allowing yourself to pass the time aimlessly.

• Studying

Often associated only with a specific test or paper, studying is actually something that is most rewarding when it's done as intended: for its own sake and on a daily basis. Studying in this gradual, slow-but-sure manner is the most effective way of literally staying on course while building a solid body of knowledge. It's also the most enjoyable and efficient means of ensuring that you get good grades on tests and papers. Procrastination *always* breeds stress and makes studying a drag.

• Taking Tests

Doing well on tests involves much more than just studying for them. It also helps enormously if you participate in the classroom experience that lies behind the tests, develop a good understanding of the instructor's teaching objectives and testing style, build your own self-confidence, and improve your general abilities to recall information, organize your thoughts, and pace your time. Procrastination can prevent, undermine, or confound any and all of these endeavors.

• Conducting Activities

Course-related activities that you may need to do can range from honing a required skill, like using a microscope or making a spreadsheet, to managing a required project, such as a demographic survey, a theatrical performance, or a classroom presentation. In any event, these multifaceted tasks bring with them greater-than-usual demands for your time, energy, and resources. Understandably, they also bring with them greater-than-usual temptations to procrastinate.

• Cooperating With Others

In order for you to master the student experience, there are many people with whom you *must* interact effectively—and even more people who might be helpful to you if you gave them half a chance. They include other students, instructors, professors, administrators, advisors, staff members, and outside experts. Sometimes procrastination forestalls connecting with these people at all. Other times, it can sour relationships with them to the point where they become liabilities instead of assests.

If you're to succeed as a student, you need to maintain a workable balance of attention among all these school-related tasks, as well as handling the tasks that pertain to the other important areas of your life. Procrastination can easily and quickly throw *everything* off balance in ways that you can't always predict and often can't manage or survive.

That's the kind of unforeseen catastrophe this book will

help you prevent. It will empower you to balance all the tasks you truly need to juggle regardless of your particular situation or procrastination problem.

Another dimension of the college experience that this book will address is dealing with the *feelings* that can so easily overwhelm you and reinforce your procrastination. Among the most prevalent emotions of this nature, discussed more specifically in the chapters that follow, are these:

- **Panic**

At any stage of a task, you may be overwhelmed by panic—the ultimate "Oh, my God!" feeling. In the beginning you may panic about whether you can do the task at all. Later, when you face the deadline, see that you've fallen seriously behind, and realize that you've bungled all your good intentions, you're almost certain to panic. Then comes a panic-driven rush to get things done. Even after you've accomplished the task (*if* you manage to complete it), you may continue to taste the bitter residue of panic as you agonize over the quality of your performance—and what it says about yourself and your prospects.

- **Discouragement**

Discouragement is the ghastly ebb state of panic. In contrast to the red-hot frenzy of anxiety, it's the desolate, lethargic, "it's too much" blues. Having realized your dilemma—and, perhaps, having noted with envy that many of your peers are *not* in the same hot water—you're tempted to give up. Sad to say, you may yield to this temptation without any real need to do so. You may be trying to avoid judgment, telling yourself, "I can't fail to do a good job if I don't do any job at all." Or you may simply be trying to jump off the roller coaster of hysterical highs and depressing lows as soon as you can. Whatever your motive, you only guarantee that the essence of your discouragement will linger to haunt you again and again.

• Resistance

Rather than feeling discouraged about yourself, you may routinely deflect your negativity outward into resistance against the task or against other people associated with the task. Your resistance can take several different forms. Sometimes it's a feeling of being trapped in a fit of anger: "That's not fair!" "He's a rotten teacher!" "She doesn't realize how hard this is!" Other times, the feeling goes beyond anger to obstinance: "I refuse to do something so meaningless!" "I'll show him!" "She's going to have to give me a break!" Whatever specific form your resistance takes, you are blocking your own valuable energy, thwarting your own good purposes, and getting nowhere fast.

So the big questions are: How can you conquer your particular problem? How can you end your personal cycle of failed expectations, painful regrets, and diminished self-esteem? How can you stop merely obsessing about your procrastination and, instead, start working to overcome it?

The answer lies in taking a much closer look than you ever have before at the specific ways in which you procrastinate.

The Six Styles of Procrastination

The first and most important step toward positive change is to gain a better understanding of procrastination as a complex *pattern* of avoidance caused by an internal conflict: You want or need to do something, but you also feel a resistance toward doing it. This is called an "approach-avoidance" conflict. Like a Hamlet in the world of action, you're torn between two impulses—"to do or not to do." You're stymied by ambivalence, incapable of making a clear commitment one way or the other.

Maybe you'll eventually start doing what you want or need to do, but some lingering resistance will make you waste a lot of time and energy as you go along. Maybe you'll remain completely stuck in your inner conflict until the last possible moment, when you finally lurch into doing whatever you need to do, perhaps with a strong push from someone—or something—else. If so, the chances are very good that you won't be ready in time. You may have to arrange for an extension (perhaps with a grade penalty) or apply for an incomplete. In any event, you will have upset your overall time schedule, and, because of your chronic tendency to procrastinate, you may keep on falling behind until you start losing courses and credits and possibly even whole years of time.

Or maybe you'll *never* get beyond your initial, self-crippling conflict at all. Your natural energy will remain dammed, and you'll be damned to yet another failure.

How do things get this bad? It's seldom due to laziness. Far from being sluggards, as the stereotype would have it, chronic procrastinators generally have an abundance of built-in energy. It just isn't flowing as smoothly as it should from mental preparation to physical execution. Instead, it remains mostly mental in nature.

To outgrow your own recurring syndrome of procrastination once and for all, you need to cultivate the skill of making more natural and fluid transitions from mental activity to physical activity, so that the appropriate amount of time and energy gets allotted to each phase. The key to this breakthrough is to identify precisely how you tend to procrastinate; in other words, what your personal, internal conflicts are.

I call these internal conflicts "BUT" factors, because the chronic procrastinators I've counseled tend to use the word "but" when describing their feelings:

"I'd like to finish what I'm doing *BUT* it's not perfect!"

"I'd like to start doing it *BUT* I hate all those bothersome details!"

"I could do it *BUT* I'm afraid to make a change!"

"I'd do it now *BUT* I like doing things at the last minute!"

"I could do it *BUT* why should I have to do it?"

"I'd do it now *BUT* I have so much to do!"

Here are the six fundamental procrastination styles that relate to the six major BUT factors I've just described:

1. The Perfectionist: ". . . BUT I want it to be perfect!"
As a perfectionist, you can be reluctant to begin—or complete—a task because you don't want to do anything less than a perfect job. You may also be worried about failing the great expectations that you believe (rightly or wrongly) other people have of you, but your primary concern is not to fall short of your own very high standards.

Unfortunately once you've started something, you often spend far more time and energy on it than is needed. This is a commonly unrecognized or misunderstood form of procrastination that involves postponing the completion of a task by *over*working.

2. The Dreamer: ". . . BUT I hate all those bothersome details!"

As a dreamer, you want life to be easy and fun. Difficult challenges that you confront can automatically provoke resistance: "That might be hard to do" gets converted into "It's too much trouble to do." You're very adept at hatching—and then championing—grandiose plans, but you often feel incapable of turning these plans into full-blown realities: a pattern that frustrates you as well as others around you.

Not entirely at ease with the practical world, you're inclined to retreat into fantasies, saying to yourself things like, "Maybe I'll get a lucky break" or "I'm a creative person—I don't have to do things the typical [i.e., methodical] way." You also rely too much on others to take care of the specific details of your life, so that you can continue to live comfortably in your head.

3. The Worrier: ". . . BUT I'm afraid to make a change!"

As a worrier procrastinator, you have an exorbitant need for safety that causes you to fear taking any kind of risk. You proceed through life with extreme caution, constantly worrying about "what if"s. When faced with a new demand, you become especially anxious because anything new involves change, which means uncertain and potentially undesirable consequences. For this reason, you avoid making decisions, or following through on them, for as long as you can. Once you finally begin working on a project, you drag it out to soften the blow. Many times, consciously or subconsciously, you do everything you can to keep from actually finishing it so that you never have to leave the comfort zone of the familiar and move on.

Sadly, you often resist change or completion even when you know that it's almost sure to improve your situation. You may wind up staying in college longer than necessary or appropriate, procrastinating because you're worried about leaving the relative security of school and fearful about your ability to make it in the real world.

4. The Crisis-Maker: ". . . BUT I like doing things at the last minute!"

As a crisis-maker, you crave living on the edge. Addicted to the rush of high emotion, ever-present danger, and emergency activity, you secretly love pulling things off at the final moment. To you, procrastination is a pathway to adventure, an opportunity to be a hero.

Unfortunately the stress that you create for yourself and those around you can become so intense that it handicaps the quality of your work. Despite the valiant marathon study session, the results on the final exam are disappointing. Regardless of all the wonderful resources you finally downloaded on Sunday, the report's just not ready by Monday.

5. The Defier: ". . . BUT why should I have to do it?"

As a defier, you're a rebel trying to buck the rules. You may be openly proud of your habit of procrastinating just because it goes against the way everybody else thinks you should do things. By procrastinating, you set your own idiosyncratic schedule—one that nobody else can control or predict. You are displaying your individuality and taking a stand against authority.

Alternatively, you may not be so blatant or smug about your defiance, perhaps because you're less consciously aware of what you're doing. You don't flaunt your procrastination. You simply say you'll do things, but don't—a form of what is called "passive-aggressive" behavior.

Whichever type of defier procrastinator you are, you see comparatively routine tasks (like attending class or doing daily reading assignments) as major impositions on your time and energy. This attitude is to your own detriment because, in fact, they are things you should take in stride—and value—as normal responsibilities of student life.

6. The Overdoer: ". . . BUT I have so much to do!"

As an overdoer procrastinator, you wind up saying "yes" to too many things because you like to please people and can't bring yourself to make firm choices or set clear priorities. You haven't yet mastered the art of decision-making, and, consequently, you end up with too much on your plate. Because of this weakness, you're also inclined to be unskilled in managing time, organizing resources, and resolving conflicts. You continually try to do too many things, inevitably failing in some way or another: You either don't get everything done, don't get anything done, or don't get things done very well.

You may well be a hard worker by nature, and may often do an outstanding job with a certain difficult task. Regrettably, these otherwise positive factors can keep you and others from realizing that you even have a chronic procrastination problem—until you suddenly burn out and crash.

Each of these six procrastination styles—the perfectionist, the dreamer, the worrier, the crisis-maker, the defier, and the overdoer—involves a different pattern of blocking one's productive flow of energy. The individual procrastinator, however, seldom exhibits only one of these styles in the overall way that he or she functions. Instead, each chronic procrastinator relies on a mix of styles: two or three styles that are the most often utilized (the *major* styles) along with two or three styles that are employed less often, but still with some degree of frequency (the *minor* styles).

For instance, suppose you usually have grandiose fantasies, like a dreamer procrastinator. In addition to this trait, you may also harbor the obsessiveness of a perfectionist, who, among other things, takes pleasure in refining fantasies to make them all the more dazzling. As a result, you may dream away hours, day after day, to avoid beginning a project; but once you finally start it, inner tendencies toward perfectionism may emerge and become the major cause of procrastination. You may also be a bit of a crisis-maker who craves working under pressure, so you may wait until you are under the gun before even beginning the task involved.

In fact, chronic procrastinators tend to harbor many—and occasionally all—of the six procrastination styles to varying degrees, with different circumstances triggering different combinations of styles. For example, you may think of yourself as primarily a defier procrastinator, especially in direct relationship with your teachers, who, in their role as authority figures, give you plenty of opportunities to feel subordinate, dependent, inferior, and resentful. However, with a bit more introspection, you may become aware that your procrastination takes on a different form in other areas of your life. When it comes to pursuing your goals as, say, a photographer, you may function more like an over-doer, creating too many shooting assignments for yourself, committing yourself too deeply with more than one photography club, and trying to gain proficiency with several high-tech cameras simultaneously. In your social life, you may primarily display a dreamer style of procrastination, fantasizing about all sorts of relationships you'd like to have without taking any steps to form one.

Learning and Unlearning Procrastination

As a chronic procrastinator, you tend to avoid a lot and may even put off acknowledging that you have a problem. No doubt you often resort instinctively to denial: "It's not my fault. It's no big deal. Everybody does it." You tell yourself that fundamentally you mean well (procrastinators generally do), and therefore no significant self-examination or change is required.

You're only fooling yourself!

In order to realize how extensively, deeply, and dangerously your own tendency to procrastinate is embedded into your daily thoughts and deeds, you have to take a good, hard look at your life. What's more, you need to look as far back into the past as you can. You are not a *born* procrastinator, you *learned* how to procrastinate as you grew up. Your major education in developing this tendency took place during childhood, and your major teachers, despite their best intentions, were your early caregivers.

For example, when I first talked with Michelle, a nineteen-year-old college student, she admitted, "I related very much to Peter Pan when I was a kid. I did not want to grow up and deal with the adult world. My parents and teachers were always telling me that I was so smart and so talented. After a while, I didn't want to hear it anymore. It gave me the feeling that I had all these responsibilities to live up to, and I just didn't want to do that."

From the very start of our relationship, Michelle was identifying herself as a defier procrastinator, in effect declaring, "I may have all this great potential, BUT I don't feel like living up to what everyone else expects of me." In college, she was continuing to fight her teachers and parents as if she were still a little girl—refusing to do things within the defined schedules and, instead, taking pride in doing things in her own time. Unfortunately, her own time for a particular task frequently had no end point; and sometimes, no beginning.

Michelle also procrastinated in pursuing her personal interests and ambitions, but in a different way. "I definitely want to write a novel someday," she declared. "It's been an ambition I've had since I was a freshman in high school. But I'm not sure what I want to say, and I never seem to get around to actually starting anything." She made up for this inactivity by continually fantasizing about the characters, plots, themes, and images she *might* pursue, and the adventures and rewards a writer's life *might* bring to her. In doing so, she revealed herself to be a dreamer as well as a defier procrastinator. The former style tended to prevail in the way she dealt with her personal goals, while the latter style took the lead in her student life—so much so that she was in danger of defiantly dropping out of college altogether before she'd even given it a fair chance.

At the close of this chapter are six questionnaires that you can use to evaluate your current ways of thinking, speaking, and acting. Your responses to these quizzes will enable you to identify your personal "BUT" factors and procrastination styles: both major and minor.

In addition to answering these quizzes as honestly as you can, you also need to examine your childhood to gain a better understanding of how you developed your procrastination problem. Start this valuable endeavor right now by asking yourself the following questions, which you can continue to ponder as you progress through this book:

• How did my parents (or early caregivers) respond to major challenges they faced? What might I have learned, for better or worse, from this?

• What messages did my parents communicate to me—by words or deeds—regarding:

  • spending time, wasting time?

  • taking a risk, playing it safe?

  • the importance of schoolwork, the importance of play?

  • the need to be responsible, the consequences of letting things slide by?

  • what constitutes "success" in school, what constitutes "failure?"

  • my own personal strengths and competencies, my own personal weaknesses and incompetencies?

• What impact did each of these messages have on me?

• What is my own viewpoint on each of these issues now?

Now that you understand the nature of your procrastination problem a little better and regard it a bit more seriously, it's equally important to take more action to resolve it. You don't have to remain at the mercy of *any* pattern of living that's doing you more harm than good. As you deepen your awareness of your particular procrastination habits, you can increase your ability to say with conviction, "No! I'm not going to let them rule my life anymore!"

Later in this book, I will give you specific, practical, and easy-to-follow recommendations for changing each negative procrastination style into more positive ways of thinking, speaking, and behaving. These suggestions will help you transform your negative "BUT" factors into positive "AND" factors, as follows:

THE "BUT" PATH	THE "AND" PATH
. . . BUT I don't want to do this!	. . . AND I will get it done!
. . . BUT it's so difficult!	. . . AND I'll give it the time and energy it needs!
. . . BUT I want to watch TV!	. . . AND I'll work now and watch TV later!
. . . BUT I won't be totally satisfied unless it's perfect!	. . . And I'll complete it nevertheless!

Conquering procrastination isn't just a matter of getting yourself better organized or managing your time more effectively. In truth, procrastination is far more complicated than that, and requires more insightful guidance to overcome. On the other hand, you don't need to put yourself through an arduous or radical makeover. Although this book will assist you in creating a more natural flow of time and energy in all aspects of your life, it doesn't ask you to change your entire personality or to do things somebody else's way—the allegedly "right" way. Instead, it guides you in understanding how some aspects of your personality may be sabotaging your best efforts. Then it helps you make the particular transformations that are most appropriate for *you*.

Continue reading, and you'll discover exactly how to switch from your personal path of avoidance—the "BUT" path—to your personal path of accomplishment—the "AND" path. You'll gain the tools to create a way of living that works *for* you, not against you. You'll master the student experience, and you'll discover that learning to live without procrastination becomes ever more inviting and exciting as you grow ever more powerful and focused.

Before you take the six quizzes that will reveal your most significant procrastination styles, I'll give two successful ex-procrastinators the final inspirational words in this chapter. Looking back on her college experience, Lisa, now a twenty-five-year-old manager of a computer services firm, concludes:

By far the most important single thing that I ever learned in college was to get as much done ahead of time as I could: schoolwork, household chores, whatever. Things just went much more smoothly for me that way. Then, when there was some last minute development—a movie came along that I really wanted to see, or I wasn't feeling well, or I got involved in a long important phone call—it didn't cause such a hassle. I wasn't creating incredible amounts of stress for myself, as I used to do when everything was always so backed up.

Over time, I developed a much better sense of what I wanted, why I was in school, and what I really needed to do to make my life work. It was amazing to me how much freedom and motivation that sense of direction gave me, compared to how lost I'd felt before. I had goals and interests beyond just partying. I could enjoy both a social life and a study life, instead of always thinking it had to be one or the other. Today I'm able to have fun *and* get things done.

Scott, now a twenty-seven-year-old stockbroker, felt that same unexpected sense of liberation when he finally kicked his procrastination habit and faced his college experience with a whole new repertoire of skills and attitudes. Listen to what he has to say:

> I can see now that there were many, many times in college when schoolwork took a backseat to something else—falling in love, family problems, hanging with the guys. When these other things came along, I thought I had too much I wanted to do to spend a lot of time just studying. As it turns out, I could have done it all. I simply didn't have enough motivation to stay on track, so it was always pretty easy to get distracted.
>
> Strange thing is, once I was finally able to commit myself to school, and throw myself into my studies, I coped with *everything* better. It seemed the busier I was, the better I handled all my obligations. The last semester in my junior year I took nineteen credits, played hockey and baseball, helped my dad with his business, and I did less slacking off than I ever had before. I also enjoyed things more. It's unbelievable what a difference it makes in your life when you tap into all that energy that you used to waste just avoiding things!

Discovering My Procrastination Styles: Six Self-Assessment Quizzes

Directions:

1. Complete each of the six quizzes as follows:

   • After considering each question as honestly as you can, circle the answer that best reflects your own experience:
   F = frequently or always
   S = sometimes
   R = rarely or never

• After completing all the questions in a single quiz, count the number of times you circled F, multiply this number by 2, and enter the total in the space marked SUBTOTAL F x 2.

• Count the number of times you circled S and enter this total in the space marked SUBTOTAL S.

• Add the two SUBTOTALS and enter the total in the space marked TOTAL SCORE.

2. After completing all six quizzes, complete the section entitled "My Major and Minor Styles" as follows:

• In the column marked "Total Score," enter the total score for each quiz in the appropriate space.

• In the column marked "Major," enter a check mark, next to any style for which your total score is 10 or above. This identifies a major procrastination style.

• In the column marked "Minor," enter a check mark next to any style for which your total score is 5 through 9. This identifies a minor procrastination style.

• In the column marked "Rank," enter the appropriate rank for each style, as follows: 1 = highest total score, 2 = next highest total score, and so on, through 6. If two or more styles have the same total scores, give them the same rank (e.g., 1, 1; 2 = next highest score).

Note: To gain a better overall understanding of procrastination, read *all* of the chapters in this book. However, pay particularly close attention to those chapters covering the procrastination styles that most affect you according to your self-assessment results. The higher you ranked an individual style, the more attention it deserves.

1. Perfectionist Procrastinator: Quiz

Circle one: F = frequently or always; S = sometimes; R = rarely or never

a. Do I get preoccupied with details, rules, or schedules that others don't seem to care much about?

F S R

b. Do I have difficulty starting or completing a project because my own standards haven't been met?

F S R

c. Am I reluctant to delegate tasks or work with others unless they do things my way?

F S R

d. Do others comment on my being rigid, stubborn, or finicky?

F S R

e. Am I critical of what I've accomplished or how long it took me to do it?

F S R

f. Am I satisfied with what I do only if it is as good as it can possibly be?

F S R

g. Do I look on my failures as embarrassments that I would hate to mention or have revealed?

F S R

h. Do I have difficulty maintaining a sense of humor while I'm struggling to do something new?

F S R

i. Do I feel upset or humiliated if I don't do something as well as one of my peers?

F S R

j. Do I think about situations in extremes—black or white—ignoring the gray area in between?

F S R

SUBTOTAL F × 2 = _____ 3×2=6

SUBTOTAL S = _____ 3

TOTAL SCORE (add SUBTOTALS) = _____ 9

2. Dreamer Procrastinator: Quiz

Circle one: F = frequently or always; S = sometimes; R = rarely or never

a. Do I think a lot about what I'd like to accomplish but rarely get projects off the ground? F S R

b. Do I wait for opportunities to drop into my lap rather than take an active, "go get 'em" approach? F S R

c. Do I let lots of time drift by with passive activities like watching TV, daydreaming, or hanging out? F S R

d. Do I spend more time thinking about the finished project than about the details needed to get it done? F S R

e. Do I long to be able to go from A to Z without having to deal with the stuff in between? F S R

f. Do I wish someone else would handle the bothersome details of life, freeing me to do what I really want to do? F S R

g. Do I find myself thinking or speaking words like, "I'll try to . . ." or "Someday I will . . ."? F S R

h. Do other people sometimes accuse me of being a dreamer, of having my head in the clouds? F S R

i. Do I do what I feel like at the moment, forgetting or ignoring previous plans or priorities? F S R

j. Do I expect great things from myself, but wonder why they never seem to happen? F S R

SUBTOTAL F × 2 = ____ 6

SUBTOTAL S = ____ 3

TOTAL SCORE (add SUBTOTALS) = ____ 9

3. Worrier Procrastinator: Quiz

Circle one: F = frequently or always; S = sometimes; R = rarely or never

a. Do I have difficulty making decisions, vacillating about what I *should* do? F S R

b. Do I need—or seek—approval, advice, or assurance from others before I do things? F S R

c. Do I have trouble starting projects or working on my own because I doubt my judgment or ability? F S R

d. Do I think things are too much for me, or worry about overdoing it? F S R

e. Do I hesitate to leave my "comfort zone," avoiding situations that might cause stress or anxiety? F S R

f. Do I become easily agitated when something disrupts my normal routine? F S R

g. Do I avoid situations that are unpredictable or may be uncomfortable? F S R

h. Do I sometimes paralyze myself before starting work on a project, wondering about the "what if"s? F S R

i. Do I exaggerate the trouble that might arise from a situation, or minimize my ability to cope with it? F S R

j. Do I think I could do more—or better—if somebody would take me by the hand and be there for me? F S R

SUBTOTAL F × 2 = _____

SUBTOTAL S = _____

TOTAL SCORE (add SUBTOTALS) = _____

4. Crisis-Maker Procrastinator: Quiz

Circle one: F = frequently or always; S = sometimes; R = rarely or never

a. Do I ignore important tasks, then, at the last minute, work frantically to get them done? — F S R

b. Do I feel that life is chaotic, and that I can never be sure what the next day will bring? — F S R

c. Do my moods change rapidly and dramatically? — F S R

d. Do I get easily frustrated and show it by displaying anger or quitting? — F S R

e. Do I act in ways that other people find provocative, seductive, or attention-getting? — F S R

f. Am I easily influenced by circumstances, responding to the need of the moment? — F S R

g. Do I enjoy—or pride myself on—taking risks or living on the edge? — F S R

h. Do I tend to get very involved with someone or something, then abruptly detach myself and move on? — F S R

i. Do I think of my life as so dramatic that it could be made into a soap opera? — F S R

j. Do I prefer action, having little patience for things that are too slow, predictable, or safe? — F S R

SUBTOTAL F × 2 = _____

SUBTOTAL S = _____

TOTAL SCORE (add SUBTOTALS) = _____

5. Defier Procrastinator: Quiz

Circle one: F = frequently or always; S = sometimes; R = rarely or never

a. Do I become sulky, irritable, sarcastic, or argumentative when asked to do something I don't want to do?   F   S   R

b. Do I work deliberately slowly or ineffectively in order to sabotage a task I don't like doing?   F   S   R

c. Do I feel resentful or manipulated when I wind up having to do something unexpectedly?   F   S   R

d. Do I feel that others make unreasonable demands on me?   F   S   R

e. Do I avoid obligations by claiming I've forgotten them or they're not important?   F   S   R

f. When people ask me why I did or didn't do something, do I feel they are hassling or nagging me?   F   S   R

g. Do I believe that I'm doing a better job than others think—or say—I'm doing?   F   S   R

h. Do I take offense at suggestions from others regarding how I could do things differently?   F   S   R

i. Do others accuse me of—or get annoyed with me for—failing to do my share of work efficiently?   F   S   R

j. Do I frequently criticize or ridicule people who are in authority?   F   S   R

SUBTOTAL F × 2 = _____ 6

SUBTOTAL S = _____ 2

TOTAL SCORE (add SUBTOTALS) = _____ 7   8

6. Overdoer Procrastinator: Quiz

Circle one: F = frequently; S = sometimes; R = rarely or never

a. Do I run around doing things, without really feeling that I'm accomplishing very much?   F   S   R

b. Do I have difficulty saying "no" to people who ask for help, yet feel resentful later on?   F   S   R

c. When I'm doing a task, do I wonder, "How did I get myself into this"?   F   S   R

d. Do I have a strong need for approval from other people?   F   S   R

e. Do I find myself complaining, "I have no time," "I have too much to do," or "I'm too busy"?   F   S   R

f. When I get unexpected free time, do I keep finding new things to do instead of catching up with old things?   F   S   R

g. Do I have a strong need to be self-reliant, and hate to ask someone else for help?   F   S   R

h. Do I get overinvolved in other people's problems, postponing attention to my own?   F   S   R

i. Do other people regard me as someone who will drop everything if and when they need me?   F   S   R

j. Do I enjoy being busy, but secretly think that maybe I don't know how to be any other way?   F   S   R

SUBTOTAL F × 2 = _____

SUBTOTAL S = _____

TOTAL SCORE (add SUBTOTALS) = _____

My Major and Minor Styles

STYLE	TOTAL SCORE	MAJOR (10 or more)	MINOR (5–9)	RANK (1=highest)
1. Perfectionist	15	✓		1
2. Dreamer	11	✓		3
3. Worrier	10	✓		4
4. Crisis-Maker	12		✓	
5. Defier	7		✓	
6. Overdoer	14	✓		2

2

The Perfectionist Procrastinator

"... BUT it's not perfect!"

What are some of the telltale signs of perfectionist procrastination? See if any of these characteristics fit you:

• Do you overestimate what is actually required of you by your instructors or professors?

• Do you put too much work into tasks, making everything a big deal?

• Do you spend an inordinate amount of time redoing assignments until you feel you've done the perfect job?

• Are you so afraid of missing something during lectures that you take too many notes or, perhaps, even tape and transcribe the lectures?

• Do you waste energy getting your desk and materials in perfect shape for schoolwork?

• Do you get too wrapped up in searching for the perfect topic for a paper or doing more background research than necessary?

• When working with other people, do you often take over more than your fair share of responsibilities to ensure that tasks are done precisely the way you want them to be?

Whatever their specific habits may be, perfectionist procrastinators generally feel driven to strive for the very best, but time after time they have great difficulty achieving it, if they ever do. Seldom are they satisfied with their work or even themselves. For all their great ambitions, the manner in which they wind up approaching tasks is usually neither ideal nor realistic.

Let's consider three examples of perfectionist procrastinators from three different points along the student spectrum: Keith, a high school senior; Jennifer, a college sophomore; and Teresa, a doctoral student working on her dissertation.

To an outside observer, Keith does not appear to be what most people think of as a perfectionist. He's not a hard worker, a stickler for detail, or even a person who ostensibly has high standards. Nevertheless, he is very much a perfectionist as well as a procrastinator. His problems are simply concealed—not only from others, but also from himself.

Keith projects a casual, even flippant attitude about school assignments, never betraying any anxiety about them as he waits until the last minute to take them on. Even then, he's easily distracted from the task at hand by any activity that may strike him as easier or more fun. His rushed, somewhat superficial work usually pulls him through in the end, but with mediocre grades. He never expresses much concern about this, and so his friends, who know he's intelligent enough to do much better, are left to assume that he's essentially a passive guy with big talents but small ambitions.

Underneath this facade, Keith actually harbors enormous ambitions—so huge that they totally intimidate him. In order to give himself an excuse for doing less than a perfect job on an assignment, he subconsciously puts off beginning it as long as he can, until there's no way he or anyone else can expect perfection in the short time still available.

Keith may not seem bothered by his lackluster accomplishments, but inwardly he seethes with frustration and self-contempt. Whenever he gets an assignment, he sincerely wants to do the best work possible. That's what he's supposed to do, as the first member of his family who is expected to go to college. His loving, indulgent father and mother expect the world of him, and he does, too. Yet he can't seem to stop himself from screwing things up again and again.

Keith blames himself for being a poor estimator of the time it takes to do things. That's certainly true, given the fact that he's never really tried and therefore hasn't learned to do things in a timely manner. But he has a more insidious problem as well. Although he longs to prove his academic superiority to his parents and himself, he feels equally pressured not to show this inner drive to anyone. If he were to reveal it in his actions, statements, or moods, any failure on his part to achieve perfection would be all the more humiliating. How does he try to resolve this dilemma—or at least get around it? He procrastinates.

Unlike Keith, Jennifer resembles the classic image of a perfectionist. She's obviously a hard worker with very high standards. Yet she, too, is a chronic procrastinator. Having completed her first year of college, she's already starting to panic about her ability to continue. Keeping up the demanding, almost ritualistic study and work routines she relied upon for top grades in high school is becoming increasingly difficult.

Jennifer's struggle is all the more exhausting now because she is living in a dormitory surrounded by other students, many of whom are very competitive academically. She feels not only compelled to study more hours, read more books, visit more Web sites, and work harder on her papers than her peers, but she also feels challenged to equal or exceed them in the most insignificant details of her academic life. She spends an excessive amount of time keeping her desk, papers, and books as well organized as possible and over-planning details for the day, such as the best way to phrase her words when making simple requests of her instructors or advisors. As a result, she never has quite enough time to achieve her lofty goals, despite the fact that she's constantly busy.

Deep down Jennifer knows she imposes too many rigid and inappropriate demands on herself, but she just can't settle for anything that she perceives as less. Above all, she fears being criticized in any context for not doing, or being, good enough. Although convinced that she'll never measure up to her older brother Steve (who got exceptional grades seemingly without trying), she's determined not to give her teachers any reason to fault her status or performance. She doesn't want them to do what her parents always did: recall her past problems, failures, or oversights as a means of goading her to improve. With this in mind, she reluctantly stalls over her homework and even her classroom tests, finding it increasingly difficult to commit herself to ideas, words, or answers that may not be in perfect accord with what the teacher wants.

Teresa, now working on her doctoral dissertation, is much more knowledgeable about her lifelong tendency toward perfectionist procrastination than Keith and Jennifer are about theirs. However, she has reached the point where she feels just as helpless to have any control over it, and just as fearful that it will keep her from achieving her most important goals.

In the past, Teresa would begin a school project right away with the goal of doing it perfectly. For a while, her strong determination and good work habits would seem to guarantee that she'd meet her objective. Then something relatively minor would happen that would throw her completely off balance. It might be a negative remark about her work from a friend or teacher, an unexpected conflict in her study schedule, the sudden dawning of a new approach she might take to the project, or a blow to her self-esteem in some other area of her life that would make her lose confidence as a student. No longer certain of doing a perfect job on the project, she would grow more obsessed with every detail until finally her anxiety overtook her resolve. She would then cease working and begin procrastinating in earnest.

In the short run, Teresa would feel enormous relief when she escaped in this manner. In the long run, she'd suffer even more stress, sooner or later having to force herself back into the work mode, with no time left to spare, merely to finish the project by the assigned deadline. Occasionally she would manage to finish on time. Usually, though, she wouldn't, and the price would be less self-regard, more need for perfectionism on the next project, and, correspondingly, an even stronger inclination to procrastinate.

Presently Teresa is stalled a quarter of the way through her dissertation. As usual in her writing assignments, she started by doing an enormous amount of preliminary groundwork, far more than she needed to do, in order to put off the moment when she'd finally have to commit herself on paper. When that time came, she realized that she'd have to eliminate or subordinate many of the plans she'd designed in her overly long research phase, among them some of her favorite ideas and journal articles. There simply wasn't enough space or time to include everything. Stymied over this difficult decision-making process, or, as she called it, her "life crisis *numero uno*," she became hyper, drove everyone around her nuts, and eventually burned herself out.

Teresa is now taking a highly refreshing break from her dissertation. Meanwhile, her future hangs in the balance. With more additional responsibilities competing for her attention than ever before, including a year-old marriage and a demanding part-time job in her field, it won't be easy for her to resume working on her dissertation and see it through to a successful conclusion. Whether she does or not, her tendencies toward perfectionism procrastination will be even more entrenched and more likely to undermine the next important project in her life.

Different as they are from each other in personality and background, Jennifer, Keith, and Teresa are all perfectionist procrastinators. In addition, they're all very smart people, but they don't effectively *apply* their intelligence to the way they function. They also don't apply it to the way they think and talk about work, which winds up influencing their final behavior far more than they appreciate. Instead of actively engaging their fine minds in the resolution of their problem, they leave them on automatic pilot, sit back, and suffer the consequences.

Why do they do this? Basically, their insistence on perfection keeps them from fully acknowledging or even examining any of their personal weaknesses—an essential first step toward implementing positive change. If you see aspects of yourself in the examples just cited, you need to acknowledge the following facts about your perfectionist procrastination:

1. As an idealist, you tend to be unrealistic in your use of time and energy.

Perfectionists think in terms of extremes: If they're going to do something, they should do the best possible job that can be done. They don't factor in any acceptable middle ground. Because real-life tasks rarely have definably perfect outcomes, the performance standards they create for themselves are usually based on personal fantasies of perfection, rather than the practicalities of the situation. Once they've conceptualized the "perfect job," perfectionists are then torn between two extremes of behavior: giving it all they've got, or giving it up altogether.

Jennifer usually opts for the former alternative, and therefore dooms herself to a sense of failure whether or not she literally fails. Seldom does life give her enough time, energy, or tranquillity to do all that she thinks she needs to do to succeed in college. By working too long and too hard on unimportant details, she procrastinates in getting the whole job done in an efficient, truly successful manner. Keith sabotages himself more directly by choosing the other alternative—giving up altogether until it's too late to do a perfect job. Teresa manages to trip herself up by going from one extreme to the other.

As distinct from perfectionists, high achievers aim for *excellence* rather than *perfection* in what they do. They define their objectives and performance standards much more realistically. In doing so, they give themselves more flexibility and broader criteria for determining what constitutes a successful outcome.

For example, athletes who are high achievers will set reasonable, season-by-season benchmarks for themselves that are designed to help them realize their "personal best." They don't set themselves up for defeat by generating a superhuman vision of perfection they must somehow attain. Likewise, they don't skip training on a day when they feel they might not execute their routines perfectly. Instead, they will do their best on any given day.

Perfectionists, looking far beyond their real selves and the existing situation, think, "I want to do the best *that can possibly be done.*" High achievers, on the other hand, think, "I want to do the best that *I* can do *now.*"

2. As a perfectionist procrastinator, you are likely to view everything in life as a burden, which makes it more difficult to perform individual tasks efficiently.

Perfectionists have such high expectations that they're predisposed to get less satisfaction out of day-to-day life than other people. They find it difficult to relax and enjoy tasks, or even take them in stride. Instead, they repeatedly turn them into ordeals by focusing on how defective or messed up things are, and how much needs to be done to make matters perfect.

Adding to the strain, they continue to brood over past lapses from perfection and to fret about future demands for perfection. Jennifer remains constantly worried, preoccupied, and overwhelmed—unable to live comfortably in the present, reflect happily on the past, or look forward optimistically to the future. Keith and Teresa, to varying degrees, have transformed themselves into chronic avoiders—fighting *against* time instead of working *with* time.

Perfectionists also suffer other lifestyle afflictions that compromise their ability to work on individual tasks joyfully and effectively. Because they're so deeply and incessantly self-critical, they have trouble motivating, congratulating, or forgiving themselves. For the same reason, they also find it difficult to accept encouragement, praise, or help from other people.

In fact, perfectionists are inclined to turn away potential allies, such as friends, family members, and teachers, as soon as they appear. For the sake of ensuring that things are done perfectly (that is, "their way"), perfectionists like to have as much control over a project as they can, whether or not they actually exercise that control. They strive to maintain an image of self-sufficiency and feel compelled to *be* better and *do* better than everyone else around them.

3. As a perfectionist procrastinator, you fear failing, and so you're inclined to postpone starting or completing tasks.

Perfectionists are acutely aware that they run a high risk of failing to meet their excessively high standards, and so they feel a correspondingly high level of anxiety. Unfortunately, they also invest a great deal of their self-esteem in how they perform. To them, falling short of doing a perfect job means falling short of being a perfect person, and that triggers deep feelings of being inadequate, worthless, shameful, and guilty. It's not surprising that they seek to avoid failure at all costs.

One method perfectionists use to try to prevent failure is to overwork. They compulsively do more than they need to do, particularly regarding those aspects of the task that are easiest for them to execute perfectly. Jennifer, for example, squanders precious time and energy keeping her desk, books, and papers meticulously neat. It's simply her way of putting off the inevitable. For the same reason, Teresa, who relishes the uncommitted research phase of a project, assembles a far larger and wider-ranging body of background notes than her dissertation thesis requires.

Graduate students often unwittingly put themselves in this troublesome position. Facing the ultimate, self-defining challenge, like a Ph.D., an MBA, or simply the prospect of life beyond academia, they balk as they never have before. Rather than take that final step, they succumb to the failings they've nurtured for so many years and, in the process, sabotage all their best efforts. In almost every case there's a hidden meaning behind the defining challenge that creates a personal conflict for them. Deep inside they're making a self-defeating statement like, "I really don't deserve this degree" or "I'm not at all ready to live in the workaday world," or "If I get this degree, I'll surpass my father's achievement, and that will destroy him."

Perfectionists like Keith seek to evade any real sense of failure by flaunting their tendency to procrastinate and then using it as a defense. At least on the surface, they refuse to take an assignment seriously. Either they don't do anything about it for an unreasonably long time, or they approach it in a very offhand, cavalier manner. Thus they hope to spare imposing on themselves their own tyrannical demands to be perfect.

According to the twisted logic that perfectionist procrastinators use, if they create a situation where circumstances are ultimately beyond their control, then they have an excuse for not achieving perfection. Keith does this by giving himself so little time to complete his assignments that he can't expect himself to do a perfect job, nor can anyone else who listens to his scoffing banter or observes his undisciplined behavior.

Among perfectionists, failure-phobia can trigger a dread of *any* change in the status quo. Ironically, even the prospect of success can be cause for alarm. They know from past experience that if they do succeed, they'll overwhelm themselves with the same life-spoiling questions: "Can I live up to the expectations that others now have of me?" "Did I genuinely succeed, or was I merely lucky?" "Does my new success truly reflect the best that I could have done, or could I possibly have done even better?"

In any case, whenever they do succeed, one consequence is inevitable. They raise the bar, developing even higher standards for the future, and their habit of procrastination becomes all the more intensified.

To appreciate how these three basic characteristics interrelate in the life of a perfectionist procrastinator, let's take a closer look at the experience of a student who finally decided to seek help for his problem. It will also help you understand more about how this style originally develops and how it can eventually be outgrown.

Jon: The Perfectionist Procrastinator

When Jon first came to me, his sole complaint was about a growing lack of self-confidence. As a senior majoring in economics at one of the nation's highest-rated universities, he felt an enormous pressure to succeed. His idealized self-image only complicated matters. "I'm truly a legend in my own mind," Jon laughed. "I always imagine I'll do things better, more spectacularly than anyone else has ever done them before."

Jon's grandiose self-image, coupled with his lack of self-confidence, indicated that he was primarily a *perfectionist* procrastinator. Other clues accumulated rapidly over the next few weeks. "I find it almost impossible to compromise, to accept anything less than the best," he once declared. "I'd rather not do anything at all than do something mediocre." On another occasion he confided, "I don't seem to get as much out of life as my friends do. Instead of just enjoying what's there to be enjoyed, I can't help noticing what's missing or analyzing how it could be better. If I go to a football game, for instance, I can't stop wondering if I should be doing something else instead, like more studying." Later, he said, "The only time I feel any sense of peace is when I simply quit working for a while on an assignment that's really been bothering me. It makes me feel like a kid playing hookey. Life seems so much easier!"

One of the clearest signals that Jon was a perfectionist procrastinator lay in the conflict that existed between his *ideal* self-image and his *actual* self-image, the latter being who he was in the real world, what he actually accomplished, and how he was genuinely perceived by others who knew him well. As we've already remarked, he pictured his ideal self as a dazzling super-achiever. By contrast, his actual self was a respectable, if unexciting, B-plus student who lacked confidence and tortured himself over completing school assignments. His best friend once warned him, "You are definitely your own worst enemy," and his girlfriend constantly told him, "You're going to go crazy if you don't cut yourself some slack!" Jon didn't yet realize one of the ironic truths about perfectionism: The more you demand that you must be perfect, the more you are likely to procrastinate, assuring that your future self will be a disappointment to you.

There was yet another important truth Jon hadn't accepted. Speaking about a time when he chose not to tackle the extra-credit challenge offered by one of his instructors, he sheepishly confessed, "I knew in my heart I could do it, but I couldn't cope with the outside possibility that I might fail. Not that there was a penalty for failing. I just didn't want to fall short of my own expectations. I thought if I didn't enter the contest at all, then nobody could judge me. Nobody would ever know whether or not I could have succeeded."

Without realizing it, Jon was defeated the moment he decided not to take on the extra-credit project. He failed an excellent opportunity to find out *for himself* whether or not he could do it successfully. By avoiding the challenge, he only wound up increasing his lack of self-confidence.

As we worked together on this issue and others relating to his perfectionist procrastination, Jon began to see more clearly how they were all interwoven. For example, one of his self-described problems was an inability to learn from experience. Not only did he fail to modify his *negative* behaviors, such as stalling before beginning a task, giving up prematurely, or holding on too long, he was not learning to recognize his *positive* behaviors, like eventually doing a praiseworthy job on a task that initially intimidated him (a sign he might have done even better if he had felt more self-confident). He once said to me, "When I get a good grade on a paper, I don't trust it. Part of me thinks the teacher must have been too stupid or lazy to notice all the mistakes that I made. I'm convinced I got away with something and feel empty inside."

Jon's dilemma is known in psychological terms as the "impostor syndrome," a common phenomenon among perfectionist procrastinators. People suffering from this syndrome believe deep down that they're never really as competent, or qualified, or deserving as they appear to be.

They're convinced that if someone were to scrutinize them closely enough, he or she would see what a fraud they are. In short, they feel like a phony.

Because of this attitude, perfectionist procrastinators have trouble trusting both themselves and the world around them. In Jon's life, this meant doubting his ability to do an assignment without somehow bungling it or being unable to shake the fear that some kind of disastrous calling-to-account would occur at any moment.

With so much insecurity, Jon was forever finding or inventing reasons to avoid his school assignments or to fuss over them far beyond the deadline. Referring to a long-overdue report in one course, he griped, "It's something I do repeatedly and can't seem to stop doing. I get to a point where I feel I've written a good report, then I find one more thing that needs to be included if it's going to be perfect. From then on, it's one delay after another."

Jon's comment that he "can't seem to stop" brings up a key self-crippling dimension of the perfectionist procrastinator's style. Although perfectionists want and, to varying degrees, try to control every aspect of what they do, they have difficulty believing that control of their success lies *within* them. Instead, they fear that this "locus of control" lies somewhere *outside* their command: either in other people, like in the hands of a professor who gave them a poor grade, or in an uncontrollable part of themselves, like their self-perceived need for perfection. Paradoxically, perfectionists still consider themselves blameworthy for their mistakes and failures; and one sure, if short-term, way to control the mistake-failure rate is to avoid completing a task by procrastinating.

All through his elementary, middle, and high school years, Jon still managed to achieve outstanding results in the classroom even if he did put off doing homework more than he knew he should have. Once he got to college and started fending for himself, however, he found it impossible to maintain the same high level of academic performance and handle all the other, more practical things in his life, like washing clothes and managing money. Compounding the difficulty was the fact that he kept procrastinating to a greater extent as the semesters rolled by. Simultaneously he was determined not only to do everything by himself, but to do it all perfectly.

"College was a shock to my system," Jon admitted in one of our early meetings. "In high school, I felt I was on top of everything. I could goof off, wait until I absolutely had to hit the books, then give it my best shot, and, bingo, get an A. I didn't see this as a procrastination problem until later, when I began looking back on it. At the time, I just thought, well, that's how you do it! So here I am, stuck with this way of operating and knowing for a fact that it's *not* how to do it, especially if you're programmed for perfection."

Advancing from high school to college, Jon also experienced another shock that aggravated his tendency to procrastinate. In high school, his goal as a perfectionist was reassuringly straightforward—graduate with the highest possible grades and get into the best possible college. It was hard to lose sight of such a simple goal, and so it was fairly easy to keep himself on track, despite increasingly frequent and lengthy periods of goofing off. Once he entered college, he ceased to have such a clear-cut vision to spur himself on.

Yes, Jon wanted to graduate with the highest possible grades, like in high school, but in what courses? And to what end? With no specific career goal formulated in his own mind or imposed upon him by the college, he was left with the much vaguer, less compelling aspiration to be, in his words, "successful in life and make piles of money."

Each academic year that went by, Jon slacked off more as his vision of the future became increasingly complex and uncertain. Now that he was a senior, he knew he had to do *something* to get better focused and work more productively. After all, he was graduating in less than a year and still had no clear idea about what he wanted to do in the future.

As hard as it is for anyone to make lifestyle changes, they are especially tricky for perfectionists. That's because deep down they fear shifting from patterns that are "perfectly" familiar to ones that might cause temporary awkwardness, incompetence, or failure, regardless of their long-range promise. Over the next few months, however, Jon bravely carried on the process of learning to live his life in a more down-to-earth manner. Ultimately he succeeded because he trusted himself and believed that there had to be a better way.

Jon adopted several modest but powerful techniques to effect positive transformations in the ways he thought, spoke, and acted. I'll itemize these techniques later in this chapter, when I discuss how you can overcome your perfectionist procrastination. Right now, I'll only mention one of them that Jon found especially rewarding: thinking in terms of a number of possible alternatives for doing things instead of automatically (and mistakenly) assuming there is only one perfect approach.

As soon as Jon faced a major new classroom assignment (like deciding on a topic for a term paper) or personal chore (like choosing a computer to buy), he taught himself to generate several different strategies for managing the task. For instance, he would consider both the notion of tackling it all by himself and the prospect of enlisting help from one or more specific friends or experts. He would ponder the possibility of researching every conceivable source as well as the possibility of researching just the most reputable or comprehensive or easily available ones. He would think about doing all of the work on weekends and, as another strategy, doing parts of it on Monday or Wednesday afternoons.

Jon's purpose in performing this activity was to train himself to think realistically and expansively about his various options for getting something done, instead of idealistically and single-mindedly about his desire to get it done perfectly or at a perfect time. The former mode of thinking offered him freedom and flexibility: "I *can* do this well, one way or another, regardless of what I feared at first." The latter mode, as he'd already found out, could only lead to insecurity and rigidity: "There's only one perfect way to do this, and if I don't do it that way, or if anything goes wrong, I'll fail."

In their obsessive preoccupation with ideal results, perfectionists are inclined to forget or leap over the type of "possibility thinking" I've just described. It seems too mundane to them. They may scoff to themselves, "Why should I bother trying to figure out another way to do something? There's only one way to do it—the best possible way." Unfortunately, they often either wait in vain for the ideal way to manifest itself or pursue their own concept of the best possible way and end up totally out of sync with reality.

How to Stop Being a Perfectionist Procrastinator

As Jon's story illustrates, it's essential for you to specifically identify your problematic thoughts, statements, and behaviors before you can take steps to overcome them. If you scored high on the perfectionist quiz you took earlier in chapter 1, you probably saw some of your own self-destructive habits reflected in Jon's story. Now it's time to examine your present and past experiences more closely to determine how you developed your particular tendency to procrastinate. Here are some good questions to ask yourself:

1. Recall at least two different occasions when you *spent an excessive amount of time and energy doing something* in an effort to get it done perfectly. (If you can, identify at least one time when you failed to get the task done despite your excessive effort.) Then, for each incident, ask yourself these questions:

- Why, specifically, did I want to do a perfect job?

- Aside from satisfying the need I felt to do a perfect job, was it actually necessary to spend so much time and energy? If so, why? If not, why not?

- Aside from anticipating the possibility of doing a perfect job, did I actually enjoy spending so much time and energy? If so, why? If not, why not?

2. Recall at least two times when you *avoided doing something altogether—or until the last minute—*because you were afraid you wouldn't do a perfect job. For each incident, ask yourself these questions:

- Why, specifically, was I so afraid of not doing well?

- How, precisely, did I go about avoiding this task?

- What feelings did I have while I was avoiding this task?

- What happened as a result of my avoidance?

The more you recollect and reexamine the specific problems you've had as a perfectionist procrastinator, the more you'll understand how severely they've shackled your life and thwarted your productivity. Armed with this greater understanding, you'll be all the more motivated to conquer them.

I will now describe the most effective strategies for overcoming your perfectionist procrastination in the three major ways that you now express it: thinking, speaking, and acting. Experiment with the guidelines for at least a month, taking care not to become too compulsive—a common problem among perfectionists. Remind yourself that change happens slowly and in surprising ways. If you're patient, sincere, and honest in your attempts to follow the guidelines, you'll discover the encouraging truth of this statement for yourself!

Guidelines for Thinking

1. Occasionally do creative visualization to become more spontaneous and imaginative.

Most perfectionists can be remarkably flexible and inventive thinkers once they free themselves from their rigid ways of conceptualizing things. Creative visualization, sometimes called guided imagery (in this case, *self*-guided imagery), can help in this endeavor. It consists of first relaxing your body and your mind, and then deliberately "seeing" images with your mind's eye that are refreshing and constructive. These positive mental images can also serve to counteract negative ones that automatically get triggered as you procrastinate. You can practice creative visualization whenever you want, but it's particularly beneficial when you feel tension that you know is caused by your perfectionism and/or procrastination.

Here's the exercise that I created specifically for people who are perfectionist procrastinators. It relies on imagining a definite, clear-cut image to represent the task that concerns you: for example, envisioning a big pile of books to symbolize all the studying you have to do. Before doing the visualization, read it all the way through several times until you feel you know it fairly well. By all means, keep in mind that you don't need to repeat it perfectly! When you're ready, perform the entire visualization at a rate that's slow and relaxing. It's designed to take approximately twenty minutes, but could last longer.

One final note: I've italicized key words or phrases in each step to help you recall that step more easily. They may serve as a kind of memory shorthand. They do not indicate any special emphasis in tone.

1. Assume a *comfortable position* somewhere that is quiet, dimly lit, and free from distractions. Some people like to lie down with their legs straight and slightly apart, with their arms extended loosely at their sides. Others prefer sitting comfortably in a chair or on a couch.

2. *Close your eyes* and take a *few deep breaths* to relax your body—inhaling slowly through your nose, then exhaling slowly through your mouth. *Let go of any tension* or tightness you are experiencing in your body. *Allow the thoughts and cares of the day to drift away,* leaving your body feeling light, your mind feeling empty.

3. In this relaxed mode, *picture the one main school-related task* that you keep working on too much, or that you keep putting off. See a definite image in your mind that represents this task.

4. Holding on to this image, let yourself *feel all the troublesome emotions* that are associated with this task. Be aware of how many different ways this task frustrates you. Notice how your body responds. *Slowly increase the muscular tension* in your arms and legs as you *let your anxiety level rise.*

5. Now, *picture this image slowly shrinking.* And as it shrinks, imagine it's not only getting smaller but *attracting like a magnet all the anxiety* you feel, all the troublesome emotions in your mind and body. The smaller the image gets, the more relaxed you feel, until the image finally turns into *a small, black ball.*

6. Notice that you are now holding this *small, black ball in the palm of your hand.* All of the harmful emotions you felt are no longer in your body or your mind but are contained inside this ball, which you are holding firmly in your grasp.

7. Picture yourself still holding this ball in your hand, but now, you are *sitting comfortably under a tree* in a beautiful meadow on a warm, *spring day.* You can feel the soft grass beneath your body. You can feel the warmth of the sun and see soft, white clouds floating across the sky.

8. Still sitting under this tree, imagine the small, black *ball in your hand turning into a helium balloon.* You open your hand and *release the balloon,* watching it rise up, up, up into the sky and *disappear from view.* All you see is the blue sky and the white clouds going by.

9. Now, you *look back at your hand*, and there's a *small pink heart* lying there. You *press this heart to your chest and feel it pass into your body* easily and magically. Imagine the heart inside of you, slowly and comfortably expanding, *filling you with a sense of peace and well-being*.

10. Now, hear the nurturing *voice of the heart* telling you, "*I love you. I accept you—just the way you are.* If you take things easy, you will get things done. You will find a way. *It doesn't have to be perfect. You don't have to be perfect.* You no longer need to be so hard on yourself." As you take in the warmth and acceptance of your heart, *feel your body relaxing, your mind feeling peaceful* and serene.

11. Continue to relax, enjoying the way that you feel. Notice how calm you are when you feel okay about yourself and about the things that you do. Take as much time as you need, and whenever you are ready, slowly *open your eyes*. With your eyes open, *say something nurturing to yourself, and believe it* with all your heart.

If you want, you can record these guidelines on an audiotape, which you can then replay whenever you desire. As you record them, be sure to speak in a slow, soothing voice. Pause for thirty to sixty seconds between each instruction.

2. Appreciate the fact that perfectionist procrastination is YOUR problem, and is not caused by your teachers, your parents, or your friends.

Perfectionist procrastinators tend to think of their problems as being "out there" somewhere. They say to themselves,

"Why should I have to ease up on *my* standards? Why is this professor making so many unreasonable demands? If others did things the right way, I wouldn't experience so many difficulties."

The sad, overlooked truth is that perfectionist procrastinators themselves don't actually do things "the right way." Their tendency to procrastinate is only one obvious way in which they're not as perfect as they aspire to be. Another indication is the less-than-perfect job they frequently wind up doing in the end. But even more to the point, the world is definitely not going to change to suit the perfectionist!

We all have very limited control over how others around us live their lives. If you repeatedly get fed up with things like your professor's remoteness, your roommate's sloppiness, or your friend's lateness, don't waste your energy expecting them to change. Acknowledge that *your* perfectionism is creating a significant amount of your frustration; and if you want to live a less stressful, more enjoyable life, it's up to *you* to change.

3. Before beginning a class assignment, put some thought into what is practical and realistic instead of what would—or might—be ideal.

When perfectionists are first confronted with a task, their thoughts immediately turn to the *best possible way* to do it, and so begins their self-intimidation. To break this counter-productive habit, think instead of *several possible ways* to accomplish the mission, then narrow down the alternatives to the most realistic ones, given the time and resources available. In making this determination, don't forget to consider your past experiences handling similar tasks: Which strategies really worked, and which turned out to be impossibly idealistic?

For example, when you're assigned a term paper, don't automatically start aiming to write a seminal paper on the topic, one that will blow people away with its greatness, no matter how much time and energy it may take. Instead, proceed calmly and rationally from the known facts: the amount of time you can afford to devote to the paper, given the deadline and all your other activities; the teacher's stated expectations; your genuine interest in the topic itself; and the resources that are readily available to you.

4. When planning your schedule, be sure to allow yourself more than adequate time to accomplish school-related tasks.

Tasks often take longer to do than perfectionists imagine, especially given their high standards. To make sure you have enough time to do a particular task, take your most generous estimate and add 20 percent. For example, if you think you may need five hours to type a first draft of a paper from notes, budget six hours. If you're lucky and you don't need the extra hour, you've got it to enjoy any way you want. On the other hand, if you don't initially add the extra hour and you wind up needing it later, you'll inevitably feel stressed, rushed, and overwhelmed.

In the same vein, when you consider the various things you might do over a certain period of time (like an evening, a weekend, a month, or an academic term), avoid imagining *all the things you ideally want to get done* during that period. Instead, generate a *realistic list of things you can definitely accomplish,* based on how you've managed to perform in the past, and allowing a certain margin of spare time, energy, and resources for sudden, unanticipated demands or opportunities.

5. Make it your goal to work steadily toward improving your grades, sharpening your skills, and recovering from setbacks, instead of always expecting yourself to get an A.

It's always a better idea to aim toward specific, practical accomplishments instead of toward some abstract standard of perfection. Remind yourself that you've got to get a lot of things done, but you don't need to do everything perfectly.

Perfectionists were often taught in childhood to "Always do your best," but, given the limited time, energy, and resources of real life, you simply can't do your absolute best in everything. If a certain task isn't very important academically, you may just need to get it done in a run-of-the-mill manner to get it out of the way. If a specific project represents a large percentage of your grade for the course, you'll want to put more into it. If it's an assignment in a major course that's especially important to you, *then* you may want to do the best you can.

Even in the latter case, however, it's better to strive for excellence rather than outright perfection. In every case except (possibly) a simple true-false or right-answer test, perfection is impossible to envision in any specific manner, much less to achieve. In the dictionary it's defined as "the absolute," "the condition of being flawless," "the most desirable state that can be imagined." That being the case, what constitutes a perfect term paper on a given topic? A perfect answer to a given essay question? The perfect student life for someone like you to lead? The perfect job for a person with your talents and interests?

By comparison, excellence, defined as "possessing superior merit, remarkably good," is much easier to envision. This characteristic automatically renders it more pleasant to strive for and achieve. It's a matter of allowing your work to prove its own worth, instead of measuring its value against some outside imaginary standard.

6. Regularly remind yourself that you have the ability to be an accomplished student.

Be your own best friend, not your own worst enemy. You need to make a conscious, consistent effort to be kinder to yourself when it comes to self-criticism. We can all benefit from reviewing our errors and shortcomings from time to time, but too much of this mental crackdown can be paralyzing.

If you're concerned about doing something that's new, very difficult, or outside your area of expertise, or if a project you're handling isn't going well, don't make matters worse by carping at yourself, thereby damaging your self-esteem. Instead, think more positive, self-motivating thoughts, like, "It will be tough, but I can do it," or "Once I get rolling on this, it will get easier."

If you're troubled about certain less-than-perfect results you've achieved, bear in mind that experiencing setbacks, making mistakes, and even failing entirely to meet one's objectives are all recurring aspects of a normal, healthy life. Indeed, they can be very valuable ways of identifying one's existing limits—and, ultimately, learning to expand them. When you're dissatisfied with what you've done, say to yourself, "This kind of thing happens to everyone from time to time. It doesn't mean I'm a failure as a person. It means I'm still on my way to becoming a success. I just need to keep my spirits up and continue to move forward."

Guidelines for Speaking

1. In your conversations, avoid using extreme language that tends to aggravate your anxiety and stress.

As a perfectionist procrastinator, you're inclined to set extremely high standards for yourself. Then you work too much to try to achieve those goals, or you avoid working because you feel so overwhelmed by them. You can help control this general tendency toward extremism by minimizing it in your conversations. For instance, if you're tempted to describe your professor as "the worst," pause a moment and reconsider. It's probably much more accurate, though less dramatic, to use more specific and descriptive words, like, "tough" and "demanding."

2. Avoid the tyranny of the "shoulds" by turning your "shoulds" into more flexible "coulds."

When you say that you *should* behave a certain way, it usually suggests that a single external standard is being imposed upon you by someone else that is too harsh or unreasonably burdensome. This kind of statement only reinforces the overly simplistic, self-intimidating belief that you have no choice in the matter, that you're being forced to conform to someone else's commands. For example, you may say to yourself, "I should change my major" or "I should read two chapters of this book every night." Statements like these imply that there's one right thing to do, and you should do it that way. In fact, you always have the freedom to choose when and how to take care of your responsibilities.

To keep from prematurely or unnecessarily pressuring yourself, replace the word *should* with *could:* "I *could* change my major" or "I *could* read two chapters of this book every night." The word *could* empowers you. It carries the adult message that you have the right, capacity, and obligation to make your own choices. Speaking in "could" terms inspires you to review many options, so that you can then commit to the one that seems best for you, given your particular circumstances.

3. Turn your "musts" into "choose tos."

Like *should,* the word *must* implies that you feel pressured by forces somehow greater than yourself to do things a specific way. In fact, *must* is a giant step more coercive. The statement "I *must* get these problems solved before I go to bed" is even more likely to provoke anxiety and opposition than the statement "I *should* get these problems solved before I go to bed."

To avoid prompting such negative reflexes, avoid the word *must* and use *choose to* instead. The statement "I *choose to* get these problems solved before I go to bed" not only reflects more accurately that you yourself are framing the strategy, but also helps you to commit to it more wholeheartedly. If you can't bring yourself to make this particular commitment, then frame another one that you *can* choose to do. The point is not to reinforce your perfectionism by getting hung up over what you feel you *must* do.

4. Each time you hear yourself say "I have to," rephrase the statement more positively: "no, I want to."

The phrase "have to" in your conversation is probably the most revealing indicator that you're imposing an overly burdensome expectation on yourself. When you say things like, "I have to get an A on this assignment" or "I have to write thirty pages over the next ten days," you only make it all the more difficult to put any enthusiastic energy behind the task.

Own up to your responsibilities and give yourself greater incentive to meet them by changing your "have tos" into "want tos": "I *want to* get an A on this assignment" or "I *want to* write thirty pages over the next ten days." This way you are truly setting goals—and acknowledging that they are *your* goals—rather than setting yourself up as a hapless victim of a teacher or parent who is demanding perfection.

Guidelines for Acting

1. Make a to-do list for each day that's short and practical.

Perfectionist procrastinators tend either to assign themselves too many tasks for a single day or spend too much time on a few tasks while excluding others they need to get done. As a result they inevitably get further behind in their work as time goes by and find it increasingly harder to sort out their day-to-day priorities. Instead of functioning impeccably, their lives illustrate a truth once uttered by cartoonist Don Marquis: "Procrastination is the art of keeping up with yesterday."

To prevent this kind of perpetual backsliding, make a short, practical to-do list for each day. Include things that are part of your regular schedule, like attending class, as well as things that are not: for example, phone calls to make, quizzes to study for, supplies to buy, meetings to attend, research to do. You can jot down the list the night before or first thing in the morning.

Perfectionists tend to plan on handling too many activities each day, which only makes them feel overwhelmed and, in the end, disappointed at not accomplishing all they set out to do. For this reason, keep your list short and practical. Guard against including everything that you'd *ideally* like to get done, and concentrate on the things that are most important for you to do, that have the highest priority. Also, resist the impulse to fill up every hour. Give yourself some unscheduled time to cope with the unexpected or simply to enjoy yourself!

It's also a good idea to use a pen to write your list, and to cross off items after you've handled them. If you write your list in pencil and then erase items, you don't have any visible—and, therefore, motivational—record of accomplishment.

2. Assign a time limit for completing each task.

Perfectionist procrastinators are too easily inclined to confuse, abuse, or refuse their time. On some projects they decide to work "until the last minute" or "until it's perfect." On others, they wait to work "until I have to" or "until the time is right." These time frames are hopelessly vague, and in the meantime other important tasks get rushed, delayed, or canceled.

To help guarantee that you appropriate a reasonable amount of time to complete all the important projects in your life, you need to write out a "time budget" for each task—or group of similar tasks—on your to-do list. For example, "phone calls: thirty minutes," "study for quiz: one hour," "internet chat: forty-five minutes," "meeting: one hour," "research: two hours."

In determining time frames for individual activities, think about your past experiences with similar ones, and then allow yourself 20 percent more time to handle unexpected developments. Any time you see that you're not keeping up with your time budget, reorganize it right away with revised times instead of simply abandoning it.

3. If you have trouble completing assignments on time, ask your teacher or a well-organized classmate to help.

Because you're a perfectionist procrastinator, you may not always be the best judge of how long certain tasks take, or how to divide your overall time into realistic chunks for different activities. If you're not sure about something, seek help from appropriate sources.

In some cases, the task you need to perform may be one that you've never previously undertaken, such as learning a spreadsheet program. If so, the most likely help may come from the person who gave the assignment or from someone else who's done it before. In other cases, such as estimating the time it takes to research a term paper on a particular topic, you may simply want a more objective estimate or another point of view, so you can consult any classmate whose opinion you respect.

4. When working on a project with other students, let each person do a fair share of the related tasks in his or her own way.

During your life as a student, you may occasionally find yourself working with others on a group project. Sometimes it's an academic one—like conducting a multifaceted experiment for a psychology class, mounting a theatrical production for a drama class, or participating in a study group where each person leads a certain part of the discussion. Other times it's a nonacademic project, like house-cleaning with roommates. As a perfectionist procrastinator, you're inclined in group situations to take on more than your fair share of tasks, certain that you can handle more than other people can or do a better job. Then, as you start working on these tasks, you wind up investing more time in some of them than necessary, and avoid working on others until the last minute, when you feel compelled to make a superhuman effort that may or may not be successful.

To stop perpetuating this vicious cycle, you need to puncture the fantasy that you can—or need to—do everything all by yourself. The more you work constructively with others, the more satisfying and productive your work and your world will be.

Every now and then, review the major tasks you need to perform at school, at home, at work, and elsewhere. For each task, think about appropriate ways that other people might help you manage it more effectively or efficiently. Then, contact some of these people and enlist their aid. Just remember: You'll have to accept that they may not want to do things exactly your way. If that's so, and you still want their help, accept it good-naturedly, not with resentment.

5. Make one deliberate mistake each day.

One of the best and, ultimately, most fun ways to break through your debilitating perfectionist tendencies is to purposefully practice doing certain small things imperfectly. In this way, you gradually train yourself to cope with mistakes and shortcomings more graciously. What's more, you learn what truly needs your precious attention and what you can let go of, without any significant consequences.

For example, if you're in the habit of keeping your desk excessively neat, try deliberately leaving it a little bit messier for a whole week. If you make your bed every morning, don't do it for three days in a row. If you're always early for appointments, come five or six minutes late to the next one. You may find out that the consequences of doing things less than perfectly are not nearly as awful as you thought they would be. Giving yourself permission to be imperfect and to make mistakes may create more spontaneity, flexibility, and joy in your life, which is a pretty good tradeoff!

6. Remember as you go through your student years that a fulfilling life is a matter of BEING as well as DOING.

Perfectionists often think time is wasted if they're not working on some task. Yet we all need time to have fun as well as downtime to relax and revitalize our energy. As a perfectionist you need to counteract the tendency to define yourself solely in terms of what you do. Regularly allow yourself time simply to be yourself. Ways of *being* include hanging out with friends, taking a casual walk or bike ride with no particular destination, browsing in a store or museum that's always piqued your curiosity, sitting around listening to CDs, or even just daydreaming.

3

The Dreamer Procrastinator

"...BUT it's so difficult!"

The ability to dream is one of our greatest personal treasures. As Eleanor Roosevelt once said, "The future belongs to those who believe in the beauty of their dreams." Some students, however, find themselves dreaming too much, and doing too little to make their most important dreams come true. They're consistently fuzzy about the details for assignments and casual about due dates. Again and again they spend an overabundance of time thinking about projects but waiting until the last minute to start the actual work. Typically they think they deserve higher grades than they wind up receiving but have no clear idea why they're not getting those grades. They also tend to indulge in what I call "magical thinking," believing they will one day do great things yet glossing over the effort that accomplishing such things would take. If you find yourself engaging in these behaviors, you're a dreamer procrastinator.

From their earliest years of playing with toys, dreamer procrastinators develop a marked preference for living in a fanciful world rather than the real one. However, as soon as they enter the amorphous state of being a college student, stuck between a childhood past and an adult future, they start lulling themselves into an ivory-tower limbo that may hold them in thrall forever. They wind up perpetually living *in* their dreams instead of living *out* their dreams, which is what higher education is meant to prepare students to do. "There are lots of things I want to do," they cry, "BUT it's so difficult to actually do them!"

Mike, a sophomore, illustrates one variant of the dreamer procrastinator that I call the "vague, laid-back type." He can't commit himself to a major, opting instead to keep on entertaining all the possibilities that interest him, no matter how remote they may be. In truth, none of these possibilities becomes clear enough—at least as far as he takes them in his own fantasies—to serve as a viable starting point for serious work. When asked about his future, he laughs and says, "I'd like to be rich and famous one day, and to really make a difference, but I don't know in what area, and I don't know how."

By his own admission, Mike suffers in many aspects of his existence from not quite knowing *how* to make things happen. It's the regrettable legacy of a lifetime spent daydreaming or acting on impulse much too often, rather than performing the work at hand in a thoughful, attentive, and self-sustained manner. He'd rather wait for good fortune to bring him everything he's dreamed about (as he's sure it's bound to do sooner or later) than take any active steps on his own to make his dreams come true.

When Mike sees a free evening coming up when he can study for an important exam, he's often initially enthusiastic about the opportunity. At the last minute, however, he's almost certain to avoid studying by washing his dirty clothes, visiting a friend to chat, listening to his CDs, or simply relaxing with a few beers.

By the time Mike finally gets around to doing the work

he knows he has to do, it is usually at an inopportune time under heavy deadline pressure. Laying back until there's no choice, he eventually forces himself through a rushed, half-baked job just to get things done. He then feels bad about himself and his work because he didn't realize anything remotely like his original extravagant vision of how things would turn out.

To relieve himself from such crushing disappointments, Mike falls back into his lifelong pattern of dreaming. "School sucks," he reminds himself. "Dreams never let you down." Or do they? It's a question he doesn't dare ask himself.

Mike's girlfriend can't help but notice how routinely he procrastinates and often tells him point-blank how concerned she is about this bad habit. But even though he admits to being a procrastinator, he can also discount her concern, claiming that she's just a worrier by nature. So, employing his own self-justifying, downright dreamy logic, he manages to persuade himself that his procrastination is a bigger problem for her than it is for him.

Marcy, a freshman, represents another kind of dreamer procrastinator that I call the "dependent, narcissistic type," Narcissus being the handsome youth in Greek mythology who spends hours at a time staring rapturously at his own reflection in the water. She has never outgrown being her father's "little princess." Because she stills resides at home, it's easy for her to continue living with this image of herself while putting off any significant progress in the real world outside of her magic kingdom.

Like a little princess, Marcy resists making firm decisions or taking timely action on a school project as a means of indulging herself. When she subsequently fails with the project, she whimpers, pouts, smirks, clowns, falls apart, or otherwise acts in a childlike manner as a means of begging indulgence from others. She often resorts to these same immature tactics to get others to do her work for her in the first place.

Marcy doesn't like the way she behaves, but she feels childishly helpless to stop it. Her overriding goal is pleasure, and she seeks to obtain this goal by dwelling as much as she can in the beautiful, self-centered, and (hopefully) self-satisfying world of her own fantasies. When describing herself to new acquaintances, she often says, "You know that Cyndi Lauper song, 'Girls Just Want to Have Fun'? That's me!" Truly addressing her procrastination problems would involve growing into a more mature identity, and that prospect scares her. Who would she be then?

Marcy doesn't bother looking much beyond that dreamy image of herself that she finds so appealing. The few things she authentically enjoys doing, like writing poetry, doing aerobic exercises, or canoeing, she perceives as unimportant despite their potential to have practical value in her life if she'd only take them a bit more seriously. Everything else, including going to class or studying, she sees as something that's inherently "no fun" and, accordingly, something she doesn't want to do.

Time and time again in their separate ways, Mike and Marcy fall victim to the enormous gap between their daydreams and their actual day-to-day lives. Dreamer procrastinators of either the vague, laid-back type (like Mike) or the dependent, narcissistic type (like Marcy) display these four troublesome personality traits:

1. **Dreamer procrastinators spend so much of their lives involved in their own mental fantasies that they tend to be passive people rather than active ones.**

Dreamer procrastinators are inclined to invent grandiose fantasies about themselves and their futures. They do this either to compensate for their performance failures or to avoid acknowledging the need to take a practical attitude toward life. Instead of being responsible about earning money, they count on winning the lottery, or attracting a wealthy patron, or inheriting money from a surprise source. Rather than acknowledge the relative mediocrity of their work and the corresponding need to put more time and effort into it if they want to do better, they sink back into visions of someday, somehow astounding everyone with the unprecedented brilliance of what they've accomplished.

Because they so often and so extensively indulge in this kind of wait-and-see fantasizing, dreamer procrastinators prevent themselves from acquiring the self-discipline and life-management skills that ultimately serve as a much more tangible source of pride, motivation, and confidence. Mike, for example, flips back and forth between spells of disappointment over poorly executed schoolwork and ecstacies of relief based on alcohol- or pot-induced reveries. He never takes steps to settle himself in the happy middle ground of a well-planned, well-executed, and well-enjoyed life.

Marcy also keeps herself noncommittally passive by living as much as she can in her own, timeless fantasy of perpetual fun and childlike innocence. Her pattern serves as a mirage to screen out the requirements and necessities of college life. She subconsciously believes that as long as she can put off facing certain realities (like class assignments), they don't exist for her. However, the truth is that they *do* exist for her, whether she acknowledges them or not. By refusing to become more actively engaged in these realities, she's already handling them in a problematic manner that will create bigger and more unmanageable problems as time goes by.

2. **Because dreamer procrastinators instinctively resist paying attention to facts and details, it's difficult for them to accomplish certain tasks.**

Dreamer procrastinators like thinking or talking about a project far more than actually doing anything about it. They prefer being swept up in generalities to tying themselves down to a particular way of doing things. As a result, they develop a willful blindness and clumsiness toward the actual who-what-where-when-why-how details involved in accomplishing a task. By cultivating this avoidance pattern, in the long run they are creating a true lack of competence.

We can see this behavior in the way Mike and Marcy insist on doing things impulsively. A task that requires more thoughtful attention immediately puts them off until a must-do deadline looms over them. At that point, they're compelled to perform it under such rushed, stressful conditions that they not only fail to learn how to do it well but also develop a dread of ever doing the same kind of task again. These two factors make it all the more difficult for them to focus on that kind of task the next time it presents itself.

Dreamer procrastinators often think that they're inherently unable to do certain tasks, such as learning how to type, or that particular abilities are beyond them, like balancing a checkbook. It's something they've taught themselves to believe that doesn't have a basis in reality. Psychologist Martin Seligman calls this pattern "learned helplessness." In fact, these tasks are simply things that they don't pay attention to, don't want to do, or haven't yet tried or successfully learned to do. Such tasks will continue to appear undesirable or undoable, whether or not they truly are, until dreamer procrastinators overcome their tendency to avoid them rather than take them on.

Meanwhile, convinced that they're helpless to perform certain projects or procedures, dreamer procrastinators tend to rely on others to do their work—or even their worrying—for them. Mike, for instance, allows his own procrastination to become a bigger problem for his girl-friend (at least on a surface level) than it is for him, thus letting himself off the hook. And Marcy frequently re-sorts to childlike pleading to get others to take on the tasks that she feels are beyond her.

3. Because dreamer procrastinators long for life to re-main continuously easy and enjoyable, they resist any new development that might be hard, upsetting, or un-comfortable.

Dreamers form a very vague concept of an ideal existence as one that always "feels good." With this definition as a guide, they imagine a reality in which they can drift through life without any obstructions, setbacks, or dis-turbances. When they do find themselves confronted with fairly involved projects like completing college-level assignments, they often wish they could handle them simply by going from A to Z without having to deal with all the stuff in between. The alternative approach—actu-ally going through assignments step by step—appears in their minds as a decidedly second-rate strategy. They don't see any pleasure or even much value in approach-ing tasks that way.

Unfortunately, their fixation on the ideal state of feel-ing good all the time causes dreamer procrastinators to lose sense of how they really feel from moment to moment, and what might, in fact, make them feel good on a long-term basis. Instead of achieving deeper self-satisfaction through taking on new challenges and accomplishing difficult assignments, they indulge themselves as much as they can in insubstantial reveries, characteristically ignoring the fact that these dreams consistently fail to offer them much growth or potential for long-term fulfillment.

Mike clearly exhibits this behavioral trait in choosing what to do with his free time. Rather than seeking contentment in mastering new assignments, he consistently resorts to the same few methods of simple, immediate, and unchallenging gratification that he's always relied upon: washing his clothes, visiting his friends, or listening to his CDs. These familiar, undemanding, but nevertheless distracting activities don't exactly make his life a happy one, but they keep him from facing how unhappy he truly is. We can also see this trait in the way Marcy lives: She just wants to have fun, but can't always find it, much less sustain it.

4. **Dreamer procrastinators see themselves as special people who deserve—and will somehow receive—special treatment, so they don't feel they have to work as hard or efficiently as others.**

Because they are inveterate fantasizers and fun lovers, dreamer procrastinators tend to be creative and charismatic individuals. This is part of their charm, and also part of their curse.

Having such attributes, dreamer procrastinators often shmooze or bluff their way through life, seducing other family members into doing their chores, talking their friends and lovers into taking care of their personal business, and conning their teachers into giving them higher grades or second chances. But in doing so, they acquire a warped self-image of being special, successful, and deserving of help that is completely out of proportion with reality. Then, when they indisputably fail at some real-life assignment, they get overwhelmed with feelings of emptiness and phoniness.

For the same reasons, dreamer procrastinators often develop a genuine but inappropriately high degree of dependence on others around them. They so often seek help in doing the work they're expected to do for themselves that they don't gain the knowledge and skills they require to function independently. What starts out as a clever maneuver to get what they want as easily as possible turns into the only way they can manage their own affairs—no matter how much trouble it involves.

Their creative bent coupled with their inflated sense of entitlement also leads dreamer procrastinators to envision unrealistic rescue scenarios. Regrettably, these scenarios make practical, important self-help measures appear unnecessary and even faintly demeaning. Hence Mike would rather wait for good fortune to strike than go out and make his own fortune. After all, if he's convinced himself that he's special, then he has to believe that good fortune will, indeed, come his way, so why should he waste time and effort going after it the "hard" way? It would be breaking the faith!

Living so much of their lives inside their own heads, it's no wonder that dreamer procrastinators lose touch with the skills they need to develop to be successful in the outside world. They also fail to appreciate how problematic their own ways of thinking, speaking, and behaving really are. They wind up living in a soft-focus reverie, which, as it drifts along, gives them less and less hard-core experience or incentive to function in a more effective manner.

Let's examine this kind of debilitating reverie more closely by considering the case of one of my former, dreamer-procrastinator clients whom I'll call "Kathi."

Kathi: The Dreamer Procrastinator

We may not be aware of it, but the images that appear on our personal belongings can reveal a great deal about our innermost selves. So it was with Kathi, a junior in college who was seeking, in her words, "someone to help me get my act together." She came to our first session wearing an attractive denim jacket. I admired the picture embroidered on the breast pocket—a hot-air balloon with soft-colored panels in all shades of the rainbow. After I'd come to know Kathi better, I realized that this hot-air balloon was a good metaphor for her dreamer-procrastinator self: always up in the clouds, going wherever the wind might take her, brimming with beautiful designs, but vulnerable to puncture and collapse in any storm that might arise.

Kathi may have been a junior, but she was in her fifth year as a college student. Every year the pattern had been the same. She'd sign up for a full load of classes, but nothing heavier than she felt capable of handling and all subjects that interested her. She'd begin the term with a big wave of enthusiasm, throwing herself into her reading, writing, and fieldwork assignments with gusto. Then the wave would somehow crash. She'd lose her motivation and sense of direction and once again feel herself sinking into a kind of stupor. Near the end of each term, she'd have to drop some of her courses in order to put all her last-minute efforts into passing others.

Describing this pattern, Kathi kept accusing herself of being "spineless" and "fuzzy." "Time feels endless to me," she said. "I can spend a lot of time in my head thinking about some assignment I need to do, but it leads nowhere. I get tired or distracted and find myself in a trance just watching time go by."

After our first session, Kathi recognized that she was a

dreamer procrastinator, but saw the problem fairly simplistically as a motivational one. "What I need most is someone to help me focus," she declared. "I need someone to sit me down and make me do things."

Presumably, that's what Kathi hoped to find in me—a kind of stern coach or drill sergeant. She didn't initially see that her procrastination problem was a fairly complex one involving a host of different ways she had learned to think, speak, and behave. She also didn't appreciate that *she* needed to be the initiator of changes before her problem would start going away.

It's understandable that Kathi believed her salvation lay in other people helping her, not in her helping herself. All her life she'd nurtured an image of herself as some sort of "golden girl" (her phrase) who was ill-suited to deal with the baser metal of real life. "I've always been drawn to people who know how to do things and like to take care of me," she once confessed. "My parents were that way. They were always there to bail me out if I needed it. And I've had very supportive friends, people who could do things I couldn't."

When I asked Kathi about her current friends, and how they figured into her desire for someone to save her from herself, she said, "Well, they're there for me, but somehow it just doesn't work out the way it used to." Speaking about her boyfriend, she said, "Zach's very supportive, but sooner or later he gets frustrated with me, and I can't really blame him. He says I'm a genius at finding ways and inventing excuses for not doing my stuff. When he sees how far behind I am in my schoolwork, he's sympathetic for a while. Then, when he sees how little I do about it, he gets upset with me, which makes me feel attacked and rejected. I respond by withdrawing and don't share anything with him, and there goes any help I might get!"

Kathi admitted that at this point in her life, when she was expected to be more independent, her friends were proving more valuable to her as distractions rather than as taskmasters or taskdoers. "I live on campus," she pointed out, "so there's almost always someone available to hang around with if I don't want to study. I don't party as much as I used to when I was a freshman, but I still party a lot. I can't seem to create limits for myself and stick to them. I've got zero self-discipline and can always be seduced into doing something that seems like fun."

Occasionally Kathi doesn't merely waste time with her friends but becomes earnestly involved in their problems. She prides herself on being a loyal and caring friend. Thus she can justify sacrificing her own responsibilities to be with others who are going through troubles. Usually she winds up staying away from her own work far longer than is necessary.

Getting Kathi to talk seriously about her own schoolwork was hard. As a dreamer procrastinator, she tended to avoid this troubling nuts-and-bolts subject by wandering off to some other more entertaining and imaginative one. When she finally did discuss it, the terms she used to describe her academic experience betrayed the same evasive tendency. She said with a wry little smile, "I call myself a sociology major, but that's only been for a year and a half, and I'm starting to get bored with it already. I started out a lit major, then got more interested in psychology, and that led me to where I am now. I know it's too late to change majors without delaying my graduation even more, but I still don't really know what I want to be doing."

Kathi's approach to writing a paper was equally meandering. "I often have big trouble even picking a topic for a paper," she told me. "My head starts feeling like it's full of cotton, like I can't think with it. Time passes. I finally decide on a topic. I'm sure I'm going to start right away. I plan to do it. I even visualize myself doing it, seeing phrases in my head that I'm actually writing down. And I start imagining how impressed my professor will be, and how I might be able to use the paper for some sort of journal article. But then, after all that, I just don't do the damn thing! It freaks me!"

Kathi opted for the same dreamlike substitute for experience in other aspects of her life when she felt she should do something, or might enjoy doing it, but deep down didn't want to make the effort it would take. One evening, she thought so intently about going to the gym that she felt she'd already been there. "I could feel myself sweating on the treadmill," she recalled. "I could hear the noise the machine makes. I could see the outfits the people around me were wearing. My muscles were aching, and I was getting so tired I felt like collapsing, and then I had to shake myself and say, 'Whoa! Stop it! You're getting lost in your own daydream!' "

Kathi remembers being a very vivid fantasizer as a child. "I had an ideal childhood," she told me, yet again using one of her favorite words, *ideal*. "We lived in a nice, middle-class house, my mother was a stay-at-home mom, I was an only child, and I had lots of time to invent stories where I was the star."

Thoughts of stardom came naturally to Kathi during her childhood. She was prettier and brighter than any of her same-age cousins or playmates, and her parents thought she could do no wrong. "Whatever little thing I accomplished, Mom and Dad believed it was great," Kathi recalled. "Whatever I decided to do, they said it was fine with them."

Surely Kathi's parents meant well, but their good intentions had some negative results. Because their approval was

so routinely unqualified, Kathi never developed any genuine sense of validation for accomplishments. Instead of
getting practical personal feedback, she got star treatment,
and so she continued to invest a great deal of her identity—
and her coping strategy—in starry-eyed dreams.

Kathi's childhood also didn't provide her with any role
model for going after what she truly wanted. Her father
had a safe, uninspiring union job, and her mother filled her
hours after housework and child care with television and
romance novels. Neither one of them was a go-getter, nor
was any other person in Kathi's small circle of friends,
neighbors, and family members. In this respect, Kathi was
all the more exceptional, the golden girl who dreamed of
being a star and was surely destined for big things in life. It
was not surprising that she now had many conflicting feelings about becoming an adult—someone who'd be held
much more responsible for actually accomplishing those
dreams.

Throughout Kathi's elementary school years, she found it
easy to do her academic work and received good grades.
After all, she was a smart girl, and in elementary school,
there are comparatively few assignments that are complex
enough to require a lot of planning. Her first real challenge
was in eighth grade, when she was put in an honors litera-
ture class. "I was totally blown away," she told me. "I
thought I was in way over my head. Lucky for me, my best
friend was also in the class, and she got me to see that I
could hack it. We'd always study together, and she helped
me a lot with my homework, and it wasn't long until I felt
like I really did belong in honors."

Reviewing this experience, we can trace an early example of Kathi's loopy, dreamer-procrastinator stream of con-
sciousness. At first she feels overwhelmed by where she is,
an example of reality-phobia. She begins steadily relying on

a friend for help, thereby revealing her overdependency on others. It's this teamwork, not her own individual work, that somehow makes her feel she belongs there (a false sense of entitlement).

Kathi was almost certainly smart enough to make it through the class on her own and prove to herself that she did, in fact, belong there. There's also nothing wrong with asking a friend for help *occasionally*. However, because Kathi immediately allowed herself to get so upset at the start, and then never let go of her friend's helping hand, she was left with a false sense of security, a hollow feeling of victory.

To people who are dreamers, such a fate may not seem so bad, at least in the short term. Over the long haul, however, this kind of experience robs people of their self-esteem and self-confidence. Underneath all their grandiose fantasies of accomplishment, they don't really feel they can—or will—do anything that's solid or meaningful. Kathi once expressed the dilemma very poignantly: "I feel I should have been doing better all these years, but I just didn't. Even when I had plenty of time, material, and ideas to do a terrific job, I wound up doing nothing, nothing at all, until someone else put the pressure on me!"

Kathi is caught in a three-pronged dreamer-procrastinator dilemma. She doesn't like structure being imposed upon her, she can't impose structure upon herself, and she craves more structure in her life! "Other people around me seem to have a much clearer sense of what they want and how to get it," she laments. "Sometimes, I don't have the foggiest idea what I want. Sometimes I don't even have the foggiest idea what I'm doing. Last night I asked myself, 'What did I do all day?' I realized I'd frittered away the whole day, and I felt so bad. But then I consoled myself saying, 'Ah, so what! That's just the way I am.' Why can't I get a grip on myself?"

Despite moments of complete despair about her lack of focus, her helplessness, her manipulation of friends, and her avoidance of hard work, Kathi knew she had many strengths. She was intelligent, vivacious, nurturing, warm, easygoing, and fun-loving. It therefore pained her to see so many of her friends succeed where she had failed. They'd go after great jobs or study-abroad programs and get them while she'd be left behind dreaming about them. At times she'd feel consumed with envy. "Why not me?" she'd think.

Deep inside Kathi knew the answer to that question—namely, that others worked for what they got and she didn't—but she hated to hear it. If a friend made that kind of remark to her, she felt very hurt. Once she was bemoaning to a friend the fact that her instructor wouldn't pass her because she'd missed too many classes. Much to her shock, her friend supported her instructor's action. "I was totally floored," Kathi said. "It felt like she hit me when I was down for no good reason. I was so disappointed in her. Now I can see that she was trying to be a friend, to make me accountable for my actions. I know if I'm not doing what's required of me I deserve to suffer the consequences. I know I have to be more accountable. But sometimes I can't act on what I know to be true. I'd rather just feel good at the moment!"

In Kathi's case, overcoming dreamer procrastination was primarily a matter of developing a stronger, more substantial sense of self and, consequently, greater self-control. She was so oriented toward the state of "feeling good" that I decided to start there. As long as she remained vague about what "feeling good" truly involved, she was destined to stay in a dreamy world where any passing attraction might be the answer.

One day, I advised Kathi to spend the week until our next appointment paying special attention to her thoughts about how she was *feeling*. Whenever she caught herself thinking something like, "How does this feel?" or "This feels good," she was to reframe the thought so that it more pointedly involved her sense of self: "How does this make me feel *about myself*?" "This makes *me* feel good *about myself*."

At our next appointment, Kathi reported her surprise at how much she learned from accomplishing this simple shift in her thinking and how effective it was in helping her make day-to-day decisions. "For the first day or so, I felt silly. It was like a Mickey Mouse thing to do. But then the second night, I was walking away from campus to the mall, just to escape having to study, and I caught myself thinking, 'This sure feels better than hitting the books.' I immediately re-said it the other way, 'This sure makes me feel better *about myself*.' And I knew it wasn't true at all. I turned right around and went back to my desk in the corner of the library. And that *did* make me feel better about myself!"

Kathi continued to make that switch in thinking as well as making a number of other changes in the ways she thought, spoke, and acted for the next few months. Slowly but surely they brought her dreamy life into sharper focus, motivating her to stay on track.

Now, it's your turn to create your own self-help program, using the following guidelines. Bear in mind that dreamer procrastinators like yourself are often inclined to start out a new project with lots of enthusiasm, then drop it at the first sign of difficulty or boredom. Keep on applying each of these simple but ultimately powerful guidelines every day for at least a month. To paraphrase Dr. Albert Schweitzer, a great dreamer and humanitarian, dreams never turn into reality unless the dreamer gets focused on reality, moment by moment, day by day.

How to Stop Being a Dreamer Procrastinator

If you scored high on the dreamer quiz in chapter 1, you probably noticed many similarities between Kathi's story and your own life. Before reading further, take a few moments to develop a more vivid self-portrait so that you're better able to assess your personal procrastination problems and how you can help yourself to overcome them. Here's a self-assessment exercise to start the process:

1. Recall at least two different occasions when you were faced with a project and *had great fantasies about doing it, BUT never got it done*. For each occasion, ask yourself these questions:

  • What, specifically, did I perceive to be the stumbling block—in other words, what, precisely, did I think kept me from getting it done?

  • What were the consequences of not getting it done? How did I feel about myself? What effect did it have on my life? On my relationships?

2. Recall at least two different times when you *finished projects, BUT wasted time or got them done late* because you spent too much time in your head dreaming or thinking about them instead of doing them. For each question, ask yourself:

  • What, specifically, was I dreaming *about*?

  • What were the consequences of wasting time or being late? How did I feel? What effect did it have on my life? On my relationships?

You have just started the process of recalling more details about the part of you that's a dreamer procrastinator. It's a process that's bound to continue now that you know what questions to ask. Let's go on now to the specific strategies that will work best to help you overcome your procrastination pattern. Be sure to give balanced attention to all three categories of self-help: thinking, speaking, and acting.

Guidelines for Thinking

1. Practice creative visualization.

It may seem counterproductive for a dreamer procrastinator like yourself to practice doing one more creative mental activity if you already spend too much time living in your head. However, once you learn to train your mind to get more grounded, you'll be in a better position to turn your dreams into realities.

The following visualization exercise involves suspending all your usual free-flowing fantasies and instead committing yourself to a specific *process* of imagination. This process will enable you to experience in your mind what it's like to turn something abstract step by step into something concrete. You can perform this visualization whenever you're feeling stressed out or want an extra boost of motivation.

To begin it now, first read all the guidelines twice, or until you feel you know them fairly well. Certain key words are italicized to assist you in remembering them. Then, silently give yourself the instructions at a slow, relaxed pace. The whole exercise is designed to take approximately twenty minutes.

1. Assume a *comfortable position* somewhere that is quiet, dimly lit, and free from distractions. Some people prefer lying down with their legs straight and slightly apart, their arms extended loosely at their side. Others prefer to sit in a relaxed mode in a comfortable chair or couch.

2. *Close your eyes and take a few deep breaths* to relax your body—inhaling slowly through your nose, then exhaling slowly through your mouth. *Let go of any tension* or tightness in your body. *Allow the thoughts and cares of the day to drift away,* leaving your body light, your mind empty.

3. In this relaxed state, *picture yourself standing on the lawn of a park, holding the strings to three helium balloons* in your hand: one *red*, one *yellow*, and one *green*. You look up and admire the three colored balloons, swaying in the blueness of the clear, sunlit sky.

4. Now, *look more closely at each balloon and imagine you see some dark, vague shape inside of it.* You can't quite make out what any of these three shapes are, no matter how long or carefully you look at them.

5. Still noticing the dark shapes inside each of the three colored balloons, imagine you *see the balloons bumping into each other, and feel them tugging on their strings.* Imagine these motions gradually increasing in intensity until it becomes awkward and uncomfortable to keep on holding the strings.

6. Now, *picture a pole in the ground next to you,* about waist-high with a hook on the end of it. You *tie all the balloon strings to this pole.*

7. Imagine grabbing hold of the string to the *red balloon*. You pull this balloon down to the ground on your left, and *burst it with a pin*. There, among the red balloon fragments, you see *a flat square of wood*. You realize it is the *floor piece to a miniature house,* and you place it on the ground to the right of you.

8. Now, grabbing hold of the string to the *yellow balloon,* you pull this balloon down to the ground on your left, and *burst it with a pin*. There, among the yellow balloon fragments, you see *four smaller squares of wood*. You realize these four pieces are the *walls to the house*. You turn to your right and *fit each wall piece into a groove on the floor piece* until all the walls are in place.

9. Finally, grabbing hold of the string to the *green balloon,* you pull this balloon down to the ground on your left, and *burst it with a pin*. There, among the green balloon fragments, you see *a small wood roof*. Taking it into your hand, you turn to your right and *place it on top of the four walls* of the house.

10. Now, step back and *admire the miniature house that you've built*. You see it slowly growing until it is a beautiful, full-size house. You *go inside and see one comfortable chair* in the center of the floor. You *sink into this chair and relax*. When you're completely relaxed, you *hear a voice within you saying, "You have done a good job. If you take matters into your own hands and work on them, you can build great things."*

11. Savoring these words and a job well done, you *continue to sit in this relaxed state*. Notice how good it feels to rest with a sense of accomplishment. Take as much

time as you need and whenever you are ready, *slowly open your eyes.* With your eyes fully open, *say something positive about your ability to make things happen, and believe it* with all of your heart.

If you wish, you can record these instructions on an audiotape, which you can then replay whenever appropriate. As you're recording them, be sure to speak in a slow, soothing voice, pausing for thirty seconds to a full minute between each instruction.

2. Each academic semester take at least one of your dreams and see if you can transform it into a goal.

As a dreamer procrastinator, you tend to confuse dreaming about what you'd like to do with actually having goals. It's important for you to clearly see the difference. Not all of your dreams can be translated into practical objectives. Some of them may simply be pleasurable fantasies, which is fine. But in your heart you know that certain dreams are ones that you really do want to achieve. You need to zero in on these special dreams and then start turning them into achievable objectives for yourself.

Dreams are different from goals in that they lack a structure of steps one can take to achieve the goal. Often they only feature isolated images that are associated with success or pleasure: a thick, printed manuscript with a handwritten A at the top, a certificate of award, a scholarship check, a great job contract. Even when you take the time to orchestrate a dream into a full-blown fantasy with a three-act plot and cast of characters, it still morphs in and out of focus, favoring the most exciting moments and skipping over the less dramatic step-by-step developments in between.

A goal involves a plan with an explicit structure that gives the planner a definitive sense of what to do. A goal consists of a clearly stated objective that you want to achieve, actual steps you are going to take to achieve that objective, specific time frames and resources you'll apply toward taking those steps and, a goal line to know when you've achieved your objective.

For example, let's say you'd like to get a higher grade in a course that's already half over. A *dream* about this ambition might include a number of compelling but fragmentary mental-movie scenes, including (1) you sitting nobly at your desk, poring over your books, a sunrise clearly visible out the window; (2) you making a statement to your instructor that earns a nod of the head and a big, admiring smile; (3) you turning in your final exam right on time, with a feeling of complete confidence swelling your chest; (4) you surrounded by all your friends patting you on the back, incredulous at the magnitude of your success in the class.

Given the same desire—a higher grade in a course that's already half over—a *plan* would be much less about you and your feelings, and much more about what you can do to achieve a particular outcome. It would include (1) a specific, realistic goal statement, like "I will change my average from C-plus to B-plus over the next six weeks"; (2) precise, realistic action steps to achieve that goal like studying two more hours a week, asking the instructor for advice on doing better in the course, or starting work on your term paper right away; and (3) definite time frames and resources for each step, like studying a full hour more on Tuesday and Thursday nights beginning this coming Tuesday, asking the instructor after the next class for an appointment this week, getting books from the library tomorrow afternoon that relate to your term paper subject matter, determining your term paper thesis this weekend, or completing your first draft by the tenth of the month.

3. When you don't want to work on a school-related task because it doesn't feel good, think instead about how good you will feel about yourself once you've done the task well.

Being a dreamer procrastinator, you are overly inclined to seek pleasure from being passive—allowing time, energy and goals to drift away as you watch TV, surf the 'net, or hang out with your friends. There's nothing the matter with relaxing occasionally, but you're predisposed to doing it far too often and much too long, and at the expense of your self-esteem and well-being.

Feeling good *about yourself* instead of simply feeling good involves taking pride in accomplishment. On a short-term basis, you may not feel good pushing yourself to study harder than you ever have before or to forge ahead on a complicated paper that you hate writing. However, on a long-term basis, the self-confidence and self-respect you will inevitably gain from doing these activities will make you feel deeply and enduringly good about just being yourself. Eventually you'll find yourself enjoying your more active lifestyle, which will lead to a genuine pride and delight in acknowledging your successes.

4. Guard against thinking of yourself as being special compared to other students and therefore not needing to do what they need to do to succeed.

Resist the temptation to engage in self-stroking reveries of being smarter, more talented, more interesting, or more accomplished than other students. This kind of passive fantasizing can easily take the place of actively doing things that cultivate whatever special talents you may actually possess.

Unfortunately, there are countless ways that you can go about creating troublesome, ultimately self-deluding gaps between your private image of yourself and your public image. You have to stay on top of your thoughts and repeatedly ask yourself questions like, "Am I making this up?" "Am I getting a little carried away here?"

For example, you may catch yourself in the middle of mentally revising a real-life experience you've had so that you come off more favorably. You may reimagine a time in when you flunked an exam, thus failing the course, as a time when you refused to take the exam seriously on principle and left the reluctant teacher with no choice but to give you an F.

Or you may find yourself thinking one thing (appropriate to your inner self) but saying or doing something entirely different (appropriate to your outer self). You may, for instance, insist out loud to your friends that you're not worried at all about an upcoming assignment when deep inside you dread it.

Such conflicts between your real self and your dream self work to undermine your sense of identity and personal responsibility. As a result, it becomes all the easier for you to sink into an avoidance pattern, procrastinating with significant as well as trivial assignments.

5. When you get an assignment, immediately begin to develop it by thinking in terms of the "5 Ws and 1 H".

One of the most effective ways you can ground your fantasies and your vague ideas about accomplishing projects is to practice using the "5 Ws and 1 H": *w*hat, *w*hen, *w*here, *w*ho, *w*hy, and *h*ow. Here's a model to help you get started, based on the dreamlike thought, "I want to get a great part-time job."

- *What* constitutes a "great job?"

- *When* will I be able to look for such a job?

- *Where* can I go for more information?

- *Who* can help me in my job hunt?

- *Why* do I want such a job?

- *How* can I get such a job?

The point of doing this mental exercise is not only to help yourself develop a dream into a solid step-by-step action plan—although that would be a great result! It's also designed to prompt you to examine a task from a number of different perspectives, so that you can start doing and moving instead of just wishing and hoping.

Guidelines for Speaking

1. Transform vague, passive language ("My instructors this semester are dumping a lot of work on me") into concrete, active language ("I have four term papers and two projects to do this semester)."

As you listen to yourself talking with others, become more attuned to the subtle ways in which you speak evasively or unclearly—the language of choice for the dreamer procrastinator. For example, as a way of obscuring your personal responsibility, you might find yourself saying to someone, "I have a cash-flow problem" instead of "I'm in debt," or "It's a lazy day today" instead of "I feel lazy." Or, you might find yourself using vague qualifying phrases in your conversation, like "I'm *getting* out of shape" instead of "I *am* out of shape."

Make it a habit to avoid this euphemistic, tentative way of speaking. Practice declaring facts as clearly and straight-forwardly as you can, so that there's no opportunity for dreamlike confusion on the part of yourself or your listener.

You may initially feel uncomfortable speaking in this new bolder manner. However, over time, it will flow from you more naturally. As a result you will experience a greater, more fulfilling sense of having spoken the truth and having really communicated with your listeners.

2. To commit yourself more constructively to school-related tasks, turn your "wishes" and try tos" into "wills".

Pay more attention to the way you talk to others about your future. Like most dreamer procrastinators, you proba-bly use vague, non-committing verbs quite often: "I *wish* I could decide on a thesis," "I'd *like to* go skiing this week-end," "I *might* decide to move out of the dorm in June," "I'll *try to* do better next term."

Let's begin with the verbs "wish" and "try to." As a means of training yourself to speak more assertively and to make more of a commitment toward taking action, substi-tute "I *will*" for "I *wish*" or "I'll *try to*." For instance, rather than saying, "I *wish* I could (or I'll *try to*) get my lab project finished," say, "I *will* get my lab project finished." This more definite form of expression encourages you to take one step further and articulate the actual steps you're going to take to make it happen—for example, "I *will* get my lab project done by working on it this afternoon and Friday morning."

3. Minimize vagueness in your speech by turning your "somedays" and "soons" into specific times.

As St. Augustine ruefully admitted in his *Confessions*, "By and by never comes." In stating *when* you are going to do something, make an effort to be as specific as you possibly can, so that you don't give yourself a blanket excuse to let matters drift. Rather than saying, "I'll organize my desk *someday*," say, "I'll organize my desk *next Thursday evening*." Instead of saying, "I'll be done with that paper as soon as I can," say, "I'll be done with that report *by November twentieth*."

Also, catch yourself whenever you're using the nebulous phrase "I'm going to" without formulating any real idea of when. If you don't curb that tendency, you'll find yourself frequently—and futilely—attempting to defend yourself by saying, "I *was* going to."

4. Don't engage in make-believe talk.

In your conversations with others, guard against using the kind of grandiose, "say it and it's true" language that so many dreamer procrastinators rely upon to artificially bolster their self-esteem. I call it make-believe talk. Here are some examples:

- "I deserve a better grade than that."

- "I'm entitled to more time to finish my lab work."

- "I'm the smartest person in my class."

- "I shouldn't have to attend class if I pass the final."

These types of statements usually reflect wishful thinking instead of reality. From time to time, there may be a germ of truth in what's being said, but that germ is too small or too compromised to represent the whole truth—especially as others may view it. What the dreamer procrastinator hopes to communicate is some sweeping, emphatic reality in his or her favor when in fact, this "reality" is not readily apparent and may not even exist.

When you catch yourself on the verge of making such a self-inflating statement, give yourself one of two options: Either don't make the statement, or make it in such a form that you can then back it up with facts. If you choose the latter option, your original statement will probably need to be rendered far less extreme. For example, rather than saying, "I deserve a better grade than that," you could say nothing at all, or you could say something that could be more specifically explained, like, "I deserve a better mark on the second essay question because I covered each of the major points discussed in class."

Guidelines for Acting

1. For each major academic assignment, write a plan stating how you'll do it and include a time line.

By outlining on a sheet of paper the specific milestones and deadlines you intend to follow to complete a project, you help make yourself more responsible and better equipped to do it. Also, you give yourself a visual tool for measuring your progress as you go along.

On the top of the paper, write the goal you want to reach and the date by which you want to achieve it. Be as specific as you can: "Reorganizing my mess of papers" is *not* nearly as helpful as "Having a separate, date-arranged file of papers in each subject by February 15."

Next, on the left-hand side of the sheet draw a vertical line from the top to the bottom. This is the time line for the project. Put today's date next to a mark at the top of the line and the final-goal date next to a mark at the bottom. In the above example, the final-goal date is February 15.

Then, on a separate piece of scrap paper list the major tasks that you need to do to achieve your goal. In the above example the tasks might be: asking my better-organized friends how they file their stuff, devising an overall filing system for my computer, designing an overall filing system for my desk drawers and shelves, purchasing any new equipment and supplies, reviewing and cleaning my old computer files, reviewing and cleaning the files in my cabinet, consolidating old files and setting up new ones.

Finally, determine logical time frames and sequences for doing these tasks, and enter each task-plus-deadline at an appropriate point on the time line of your original goal sheet. You may find it helpful to break down certain major tasks into minor tasks and put deadlines for these minor tasks on the time line as well.

2. Use a big, easily seen calendar to keep track of your day-to-day academic and social responsibilities, and refer to it daily.

A well-maintained calendar doesn't just help remind you what you need to do each day. It also gives you the inspirational feeling that you've already begun taking charge of your life. Indeed you have!

Buy a calendar that allows you to see a whole week at a time, with plenty of space each day to record items in particular time slots. Keep this calendar in a handy, highly visible spot. Write down the things you need to do as soon as you commit to them. For each daily entry, include the specific time when you will do it.

Be sure to incorporate into your calendar any goal-related milestones, deadlines, and events (see the discussion of time lines above) as soon as you've established them. Also, block out specific periods of time each day that you seriously plan to study.

Refer to this calendar *at least* twice every day, at the beginning and at the end. Mark off each item as soon as it's completed. And don't forget to check out next week's entries a couple of days in advance!

3. Every day, create two lists of tasks: a "to-do" list, and a "plan-to-do" list.

On your "to-do" list, write down tasks that you're definitely committed to doing that day (consult your calendar and add any other important tasks that may not be there). Then refine each task listing so that it's as action-oriented as possible, with specific references to how you're going to do it. For example, if one item on the list taken from your calendar reads "4–5 P.M.: study physiology," refine it so it reads, "4–5 P.M.: study pp. 210–240 in the physiology text at the library."

On your plan-to-do list, write down tasks that you're considering doing—either that day (if you have time) or in the near future—but that may require more time or thought. Express such tasks as specifically as possible, making clear what requires further thinking: e.g., "determining what questions I need to ask to clarify my fieldwork" instead of just "preparing for the research project," or "looking for a studio apartment close to campus for the spring term" instead of just "finding another place to live."

The point of keeping two separate lists rather than one composite list is to train yourself to distinguish between things that you're definitely committed to *doing* on a particular day and things that you *plan to do* sometime soon. Dreamer procrastinators are inclined to let most things drift into the latter category, whether or not it's appropriate to do so!

Finally, don't forget to cross off items on either list *when they're completed*. It will help reinforce your sense of accomplishment.

4. Every week, assign yourself at least one special "to-do" task—something that contributes to your long-range goals—in addition to your ordinary responsibilities.

Examples of "ordinary tasks" are (in abbreviated form) "get a haircut," "review my physics notes," "return phone calls," "get oil changed in Nissan." Examples of "special tasks" include "visit the science museum to see if they have material for my anthropology project," "call Jan to talk about job possibilities this summer," "surf the Web for more information about my hobby."

Because you're a dreamer procrastinator, you need to make a special effort to get your ordinary responsibilities completed on time, so it's a good idea not to let a day go by without keeping up with your current obligations. It's also important, however, to attend to new matters so that you can get ahead (such as looking into a summer job before it's summer). This way you ensure that what's important to

Santa Clara County Library District

408-293-2326

Checked Out Items 8/16/2018 15:56
XXXXXXXXXX8449

Item Title	Due Date
1. Beat procrastination and make the grade : the six styles of procrastination and how students can overcome them 33305014689164	9/6/2018

No of Items: 1

Amount Outstanding: $7.50

24/7 Telecirc: 800-471-0991
www.sccl.org
Thank you for visiting our library.

you as an individual doesn't get ignored or lost in the shuffle. For this reason it's wise to schedule at least one "special" task each week (or more often if it's not a busy week) that will assist you in turning one of your dreams into a reality.

5. Find ways to remind yourself to get going on an assignment, instead of just passively waiting until the spirit moves you.

The dreamer in you may balk at the prospect of relying on mechanical aids to spur yourself into action. Nevertheless, you do need motivational help, and alarms, timers, and beepers may be all it takes to make a big difference. For example, if you're just hanging out with your roommate but have promised yourself you'll begin your art project by 2 P.M., set your watch to beep at 2 P.M. The mere act of setting the alarm may be the beginning of being more time-focused and committed to the work at hand.

Also, consider asking someone else to be your reminder on certain specific occasions, as long as it isn't too much of an imposition on him or her. But remember: Guard against overusing other people as timekeepers or you may never learn to assume that responsibility for yourself.

6. As a dreamer, be cautious of falling into too many passive activities and instead deliberately engage yourself in more active ones.

Rather than passively lounging in bed, smoking a joint, watching TV, or listening to music all the time, experiment with more physically vigorous activities, so that you'll condition yourself to *do* instead of simply to *think*. If you feel very out of touch with your body, you may find it helpful to look each day for separate things you can do with your *hands, mouth,* and *feet.* Here are some examples:

- **Hands:** type a letter, sort through old files, paint a cabinet

- **Mouth:** telephone a friend, sing in the shower, recite out loud some new facts you've recently learned

- **Feet:** walk to the store instead of driving, jog to class, do leg-lifts

7. Avoid being a loner by pushing yourself to have constructive interaction with other students and faculty members.

If you're inclined to stay by yourself in your own little dream world, make a specific effort to get more involved with other people in doing academic work. Get together with a group to study or quiz each other on test questions, talk to people you respect about your current plans or courses you might take in the future, ask your classmates how they're handling the course requirements.

Other people can directly or indirectly give you fresher, more realistic perspectives on student life, as well as motivational boosts. Dreamer procrastinators often suffer from their own dreamlike insularity. You could be fooling yourself far more than you realize about what's true or false, harmful or helpful, possible or impossible, difficult or easy. The only way to find out if others see things the way you do is to check your perceptions against theirs.

4

The Worrier Procrastinator

"...BUT I'm afraid to make a change!"

"**P**rocrastination is like a credit card," claims comedian Christopher Parker. "It's a lot of fun until you get the bill." Well, it may be that way for some procrastinators; but if you're the worrier type, you know that it's sheer distress from the scary beginning until the increasingly dreaded end.

As you face each new task you're plagued by doubts about how to handle it. After you finally make a decision, you continue to second-guess it. You quickly get caught up in a spiral of thinking too much; and the more you think, the more apprehensive you become. Your mind keeps anticipating the worst, and you never feel self-confident about your ability to cope. Instead, you're always looking nervously toward friends for help and reassurance rather than trying to figure out things for yourself. As a general rule you hate risk, change, and surprises, and you're only really happy when you're feeling completely safe and secure.

It's true that every student occasionally worries about the future: How am I going to do well in this course? Is my application good enough? Will the weekend turn out the way

I hope? It's also true that every act of procrastination, no matter what style, brings with it a certain amount of uneasiness about the consequences. Worrier procrastinators, however, are remarkable for the greater-than-normal extent and severity of their fear. They suffer from what I call the "Ohmygod!" syndrome. Virtually every project or event they need to face is viewed as a potential catastrophe.

In comparison to other people, worrier procrastinators have a very narrow comfort zone. They feel safe only as long as they follow their usual, predictable routines. However, as soon as they're called upon to deal with a new challenge, they start panicking, regardless of whether it's a major issue, like taking a scholarship exam or winning back the love of their life, or a minor one, like writing a short essay or going out on a first date.

Worrier procrastinators focus almost exclusively on negative possibilities rather than positive ones. Their focus quickly becomes microscopic: Every little fear relating to a new project looms so large to them that the task itself, whether big or small, becomes thoroughly intimidating. In response to this, their primary concern is not so much how to get the task done effectively, but rather how to avoid change or risk as much as possible so that they can remain securely within their comfort zone. It's a lot of work doing all that worrying, and what makes it worse is that it accomplishes nothing. Instead, it usually leaves the worrier all the worse for wear and the new challenge all the more menacing.

There are two basic kinds of worrier procrastinators: the nervous, self-paralyzing type and the passive, dependent type. Heather, a nineteen-year-old college sophomore, represents the former. She's always thought of herself as a "bundle of nerves" and freely admits that she can't work under pressure. "I let things get to me right away. Instead of just plowing ahead with my homework, I sit in my room and worry about it. I'm grouchy, I eat everything in sight, I can't sleep. I exhaust myself even though I'm not really doing anything!"

Heather *does* let things paralyze her. She agonizes over situations and their possible bad outcomes until she's all tied up in mental, emotional, and behavioral knots. Rather than making a difficult telephone call, she decides to put it off until she feels more self-confident. That moment, of course, never comes. Ironically, if she calls at all, it's usually at the last possible moment when she's at her most desperate! Her insecurities also create a nagging need to know more details about her classroom assignments than her instructors say when they announce them. Unfortunately, she's usually so concerned about bothering them or appearing foolish that she never asks her questions. In the end, when she doesn't do as well as she thinks she should have, she comes to see it as *their* fault for not giving her enough direction.

As a nervous, self-paralyzing procrastinator, Heather primarily agonizes over *situations*. She lacks faith in how they'll develop, whether they'll work out the way she wants them to, and if they'll ever get done. In contrast, the passive, dependent type is mainly worried about *self*: Am I doing the right thing? Can I really pull this thing off?

Scott, a passive, dependent procrastinator, is a twenty-one-year-old junior. His biggest difficulty is making decisions. His second biggest is following through on them once he makes them. "I'm at the point where I absolutely have to choose a major," he says, "and I still can't do it. I keep thinking if I make a bad choice it will ruin my whole life."

Unfortunately, Scott gets just as rattled by small decisions. When he's unsure how to prepare for his midterms, he frets over his options until he has no choice but to cram the night before. Thinking it might be a good idea to throw a party, he dithers endlessly over what kind of party, whom to invite, and how much money to spend, so it never happens. For weeks prior to registration, he can't make up his mind about what courses to take, so he lets his best friend decide for him as they're waiting in line to sign up.

Because he lacks self-confidence, Scott is immediately and consistently attracted to the deceptive security of doing nothing at all. By avoiding decisions, he renders himself more insecure than ever. He hates uncertainty yet cultivates it. He wants to be able to trust himself but puts himself in such a bind that he's forced to rely on someone (like his best friend) or something (like the final moment) to stir him into action.

Most individual worrier procrastinators demonstrate some characteristics of each type in the ways they create trouble for themselves. Here are four basic characteristics all worrier procrastinators have:

1. **Preferring the safety of the known to the risk of the unknown, worrier procrastinators are highly resistant to change.**
Worrier procrastinators may secretly yearn for the excitement of new things to do, new places to go, and new people to meet. However, when they're actually confronted with new things, places, or people, their excitement tends to curdle into anxiety. As far as day-to-day life goes, anything that's not familiar is frightening, and anything frightening is something they don't want to do.

Rather than grow by facing new challenges, worrier procrastinators prefer to remain as they are. If that means being alternately bored, dissatisfied, or unhappy, so be it; it's better for them than going through something risky. Their cautionary motto is "What If?" What if they don't enjoy it? What if they fail? What if something embarrassing happens? What if the choice they've made is the wrong one?

Meanwhile they stay put, spinning ever more solid cocoons for themselves out of their ever thicker threads of doubt. In the process, they rob themselves of many good opportunities to break out of their cocoons, spread their wings, and fly. We see this in the way Heather holes up in her room and allows worry to overwhelm her. We also see it in the way Scott lets outside people and circumstances take control over his own life instead of doing so himself.

2. Fearing to make mistakes, worrier procrastinators tend to avoid, delay, or prolong doing tasks.

Whether worrier procrastinators lack faith in themselves or in life as a whole, they're terrified at the prospect of doing something "wrong." They don't just mean morally or ethically bad; in fact, this issue rarely bothers them. Their definition of "wrong" covers a much vaster territory: *anything* that's uncomfortable, inaccurate, dangerous, inappropriate, unorthodox, chancy, ineffective, unnecessary—the list goes on and on.

When a new project presents itself, worrier procrastinators build up so much fear over all the "wrong" things that might happen that they often can't help shunning the project altogether, or else postponing serious work on it for as long as they can. Heather, for example, turns a difficult phone call into a repellant nightmare by imagining all the things that *might* go wrong. Scott puts off studying for his midterms because he's consumed with worry that he'll "do it wrong."

3. **Apart from being indecisive in general, worrier procrastinators fail to commit themselves to the specific decisions they do make.**

Worrier procrastinators crave the security of keeping all their options open. They hate to rule out one set of possibilities in favor of another. When the situation compels them to do so—when they finally must make a choice one way or the other—they still can't stop thinking about the alternatives, or feeling their predecision anxiety. They may determine what they're going to do, but they don't put all their energy behind their decision. They stay ready to hold back or withdraw if things don't go smoothly.

For example, Heather makes a tentative commitment to studying by staying in her room with her books, and telling herself that's what she needs to do, but she still has difficulty focusing her energies on the assigned text. Worrying interferes with her ability to concentrate and absorb information. It leaves her feeling that the time spent studying was hardly worthwhile. This is an accurate feeling: In the end, she's almost as unprepared as she was before she decided to study. It's no wonder she thinks that nothing ever works out right for her!

Scott shows the same brand of halfhearted, doomed-from-the-start commitment in registering for classes. Instead of choosing his courses himself, he passively allows a situation to develop where his best friend makes his decisions for him. Thus, consciously or subconsciously, he can later justify backing away from them. After all, he wasn't the one who picked them in the first place!

4. **Worrier procrastinators seek an exorbitant amount of advice, reassurance, nurturance, and help from others.**

Because of their anxiety, indecisiveness, and inefficiency, worrier procrastinators constantly look for support from others, especially from people who seem to be more self-confident and effective in managing their lives. In this respect they're like children, looking for substitute parents to adopt them.

In reality, our friends, teachers, advisors, and coworkers are *not* our parents. If we rely on them too heavily to make our decisions or take over our own responsibilities as adults, we jeopardize not only our own growth, but the health of all our relationships.

We see Heather pursuing this dependent course in the way she expects her teachers to anticipate and meet her needs instead of letting her teachers know what she requires or acting on her own sense of what's best. This dangerous dependency tendency is even more apparent in the way Scott passively maneuvers his best friend into making his course selections.

All worrier procrastinators suffer from each of these four characteristics to some degree. However, they don't always appreciate how strongly these characteristics can interact to compromise their happiness and well-being. To gain a better understanding, let's examine the case of one of my clients Melissa, a twenty-two-year-old college senior planning to go to law school.

Melissa: The Worrier Procrastinator

When I met Melissa for the first time, I could already see signs of insecurity. Despite her good looks and the fashionable way she was dressed, things that might have bolstered her self-confidence, she was clearly anxious and distressed. She had difficulty looking me in the eyes, fearing that I would be a judge who would soon pass sentence on her failings. Her opening remarks made it clear that she was ac-

tually depending on me to make a judgment she couldn't—
or wouldn't—make for herself.

"Please tell me what's the matter with me!" she said,
obviously distraught. "I have no control over my life. I
promise myself I'll study in the evening, but then I don't.
It's not that I have fun or anything. I just get so frantic over
what I've got to do for class that I go into a kind of trance.
My book's open in front of me, but I can't focus on what
I'm reading. I sit there like a zombie, watching time waste
away."

Like procrastinators in general, Melissa was claiming
to be—and probably genuinely feeling—powerless to stop
herself from behaving ineffectively. And like worrier procrastinators in particular, she was relying on me not only to
decide what this meant, but to take care of it for her.

By the time I met Melissa her troubles had become more
than emotional. Many times when Melissa panicked over
an upcoming assignment, she wouldn't just "sit there like a
zombie" to avoid facing it. Instead she would engage in
physically unhealthy activities. "I often pig out on cook-
ies," she confessed. "I've gained twenty pounds since my
sophomore year. I drink way too much coffee. And I don't
sleep well. Many nights I find myself staying awake obsessing all the things I'm afraid of, even though I know it
doesn't do a bit of good."

Aside from emotionally and physically hurting herself
with her bad habits, Melissa was also harming her academic career. Her grade-point average was still respectable,
but it had steadily declined since her freshman year thanks
largely to her erratic study schedules and paper grades
marked down for lateness.

In addition, Melissa was repeatedly throwing away opportunities for success not only during college, but also afterward. For example, six months prior to our meeting, one

of her professors told her about a great part-time job in a prestigious law firm. The woman offering the job was the professor's close friend, and Melissa was virtually assured of getting the job if she called and expressed interest.

"When I left the professor's office I was ecstatic," Melissa recalled, "but then I got so nervous about phoning the woman I'd be working for that I kept putting it off, and putting it off, as long as I felt I could. Each time I told myself I had to do more research on the firm, or think more about how I was going to present myself, or revise my résumé. By the time I finally called, it was too late. Now I wonder if I waited until I *knew* it would be too late so I wouldn't be rejected, or wouldn't blow the job somewhere down the line. What have I got now to show for all my obsessing? One more disappointment!"

Melissa's life as a student had long revolved around her concern about safety. Throughout elementary school, junior high, and high school, she had performed well on tests and papers, but had never allowed herself to take any major risks.

"I always aimed toward doing exactly what the teacher expected," Melissa once told me. "I never really thought for myself, or deliberately chose something hard to do, or did anything particularly creative. As much as I could, I tried to be safe. My art projects in grade school were always simple and pretty. My reports were nice and neat. I spent a lot of time and effort to make sure there were no mistakes, and there weren't, but everything was sort of ordinary. Of course, that helped make me feel I wasn't anything special, and so I had to worry every time about doing an acceptable job."

In high school, Melissa managed to stay on top of her assignments and even won several academic awards, but she still couldn't shake her self-image as a person who constantly needed to worry about succeeding. "On the surface I felt happy about being a good student," she recalled, "but deep down I still felt unsure of myself. I didn't let myself take any chances, so I missed out on things I might have liked a lot. I wouldn't sign up for Russian class because I thought it would be too hard. I didn't write for the student magazine, even though I wanted to, because I didn't want to appear egotistical. I didn't do a special video I'd imagined doing because I was worried the process itself would be too intimidating."

I had to point out to Melissa how often she said, essentially, that she was "afraid of being afraid," and what a vicious cycle this self-perpetuating attitude had been creating in her life. She was choosing what to notice or ignore, believe or deny, do or not do with the express purpose of maintaining *familiar* ways of thinking, speaking, and behaving. Even when her ways were self-defeating, they were predictable and, therefore, had the appearance of being easier and safer. Nevertheless, one important factor she was ignoring, denying, and minimizing was the downward spiral her life was taking as she clung to her practice of worrier procrastination.

Melissa was briefly jolted into greater self-awareness when she first began college. "Living on my own a thousand miles away from my family, was a big shock to me," she admitted. "I am the youngest in a large family where I always had someone to turn to when I was growing up, particularly my mom. Come what may, she'd be there to help me do things or to calm me down so that I could do them. My first year in college, I had no choice but to do things for myself, even though it was hard!"

It may have been hard, but Melissa did it, and she did it well. She earned the same high grades she'd had in her senior year of high school, even though surveys show that most college students initially get lower grades. If Melissa had continued performing her college assignments in the same determined, self-aware, and self-reliant way, she would have met with a lot more success. Unfortunately, she soon sank back into her worrier-procrastinator funk.

Melissa described that funk very well, admitting how much time she'd spent experiencing it: "I can feel myself freeze up whenever something big is assigned. I start imagining how I'll do it, but at the same time I realize I'm fooling myself. I know I'm just going to keep postponing whatever schedule I create. I'm so anxiety ridden that I can't simply go with the flow, like my friends tell me to. I forget that I'm smart and capable. Instead, I envision the worst, like completely screwing up for no reason at all. I tell myself I should start working on the assignment early because I can't stand working under pressure, then I go ahead and procrastinate anyway. It's a real paradox. The pressure I want to avoid actually revs up the moment I begin thinking about it!"

As Melissa continued through school, she steadily grew to distrust herself and her plans, developing a very debilitating condition called "anticipatory anxiety." This is a type of anxiety in which one experiences greater fear *before* an event than when the event actually occurs. She maintained this condition by ruminating over all the "what ifs" relating to the event: What if I can't find enough information for my term paper? What if I don't understand the information I find? What if my teacher doesn't interpret it the same way I do? What if I get sick before I finish the paper? What if my teacher thinks I'm an idiot?

Melissa's worrier procrastination affected other areas of her life besides academic performance. "The simplest things can get to me," she confessed. "I'm talking about things like organizing the photos I've stuffed into drawers, or writing letters to my friends from high school. I think about these things many times, and I feel I really want to do them, but I procrastinate so long that they start to seem like humongous tasks. Then I only want to avoid them!"

In fact, Melissa's tendencies to worry and to procrastinate affected *every* aspect of her life, including her personal relationships. "I'm bad at making decisions anyway, but it's a terrible problem in my love life. I'm afraid to change anything, so I only do it when I'm forced to. My freshman year, I was looking for a strong guy to bring me out more, and I met Mike, who seemed just right for me. But it didn't work out at all like I'd hoped. Instead of making me more adventurous, he completely took me over. I became a robot, with no identity and no voice. I knew I needed to get rid of him about two months into the relationship, but I was nervous about how to do it, about how he'd feel, about being alone. I waited two years until *he* finally dumped *me*."

In Melissa's non-romantic relationships, she also exhibited anxiety relating to low self-esteem and overdependency. "I sometimes feel driven by this fear that defies logic," she told me. "I'll be going along fine, and something minor comes up that I don't want to deal with. Then I'll suddenly be in desperate need of a friend to tell me what to do, to reassure me, to treat me almost like a baby. Even if my friend doesn't mind, I wind up hating myself for being so insecure. And sometimes, my friend gets fed up too!"

Melissa's most recent experience of this kind involved her law school applications, which she was still obsessing over. "I should have finished my applications long before now," she said. "A few weeks ago, I was so sick of seeing them spread out all over my desk that I begged my friend Tracy to help me, even though I could tell she really didn't want to. I know one reason I'm avoiding them is I don't think I'll get into the schools I've picked, so why bother?"

Melissa's opinion that she wouldn't get into the schools she'd chosen was based on fear, not the facts. At some level, right or wrong, she did believe she had a chance for these schools. True, she wasn't applying to the highest-level schools she'd once been advised to consider: Her grades had fallen too far since then because of her habitual procrastination. Maybe this self-engineered setback was giving her a sense of despair and defeatism about law school in general. Or maybe she was simply following a pattern she'd developed in childhood: nursing a pessimistic attitude toward *any* major task that seemed difficult or that threatened to change her status quo.

Referring to the law school applications, Melissa said, "I approached them the same way I approach my essay assignments: spend far too much time on the easy parts so I can postpone working on the difficult ones. Just like a kid with her mother, I was asking Tracy to make me do what I couldn't bring myself to do."

Melissa was no fool. She realized that it would have been much smarter to invest more of her time on the difficult parts of the applications than the easy ones. But she couldn't resist following her standard mode of operation: worrying herself to the point where she felt justified in bringing in outside help.

From Melissa's point of view this painful, convoluted strategy appeared to be the only way she was able to get her work done—asking for help out of weakness ("I can't do it"), not out of strength ("Let's collaborate!"). She said, "I felt so stupid and immature having Tracy walk me through my applications, holding my hand, that I finally let her off the hook and went on to complete it myself. So I did get around to tackling the hard parts after all, but it took so much effort, and it was so humiliating. I was hoping Tracy would do what Mike used to do—take over. I hated

Mike for that, and now I'm hating myself for making it happen again."

Despite her considerable achievements, Melissa lived in a world where many things seemed too much for her to handle. Her initial impulse was to abandon prematurely any hope about accomplishing her goals. She summed it up for me this way: "I feel anxious about my future, disappointed about my past, and depressed about my present. My lack of confidence in myself and in life is totally terrible."

Despite Melissa's disappointment over her past behavior, her resistance to change not only made it harder for her to tackle new projects, but also blocked her creativity, thwarted her spontaneity, and kept her from trying new approaches.

For example, one day Melissa said, "I tell myself that I have to study in big blocks of time, that it's the best, the *only* way to get things done. So I try to put myself through a whole day of studying against my will, which is so painful that I can't study again for a week. I know other students will study for a half hour here, an hour there, and enjoy themselves in between, but I don't seem to have that flexibility."

When I asked Melissa exactly how she went about studying all day that made it so painful, she replied, "First I need to look everything over. It's as if my eyes are too jumpy to settle anywhere, so I have to get them slowly acclimated to all of it before going on. When I feel I've calmed myself down enough to begin, I waste another big chunk of time fussing around with details, like getting my notes, desk, and books in order. Then I finally bore into the material, soon grow tired of that, get distracted, and have to start up the whole process all over again." It was as if she were trying to study with clenched fists, jittery eyes, and a rigid mind!

Despite all of Melissa's troubles, she now had one, critical factor in her favor: She *knew* she needed to make serious changes if she was going to have a happy, productive life. To her surprise and delight, the changes weren't the highly complicated, hugely difficult rehabilitative measures she'd envisioned and dreaded. Instead, they were relatively simple, easy twists in her day-to-day life that started unravelling the bad habits she'd spun for herself.

One change Melissa made was in the way she mentally processed each new challenge. She learned to approach the challenge with two distinct steps: first, commit to taking it on; and second, figure out *how* to accomplish it. Previously, she'd get hung up right away on all the work a challenge might involve, overlooking her commitment itself. Now she was beginning with a clear-cut commitment and reinforcing it by saying to herself, "Yes, I will get the task done, whatever it takes." In this manner she was assuming personal responsibility and building the ability to be her own best motivator.

A number of other equally easy, commonsense steps are effective in breaking lifelong patterns of worrier procrastination. Let's look at what you can do to help yourself.

How to Stop Being a Worrier Procrastinator

Before you take any specific steps, it would be helpful for you to deepen your understanding of the experiences you've had as a worrier procrastinator. If you develop a clear image of how you've created unnecessary obstacles for yourself in the past, it will help you progress more smoothly toward what you want to accomplish in the future. Here's a self-assessment exercise to get you started:

1. Recall at least two different occasions when you were faced with *something you wanted or needed to do BUT*

never did because you were afraid. For each occasion, ask yourself these questions:

- What, specifically, was I afraid of?

- What were the consequences of my not doing it? How did I feel? What effect(s) did it have on my life? On my relationships?

2. Recall at least two different occasions when you *finished a project, BUT wasted time or got it done late* because of excessive fears or worries. For each occasion, ask yourself these questions:

- What, specifically, were my fears and worries?

- What were the consequences of wasting time or being late? How did I feel? What effect(s) did it have on my life? On my relationships?

Using your responses to these questions as catalysts, you can proceed to recall other times when you allowed fears to compromise your success. The more you understand about these experiences, the better equipped you'll be to resist the temptation to procrastinate. Follow each of these guidelines to change the self-destructive ways you think, speak, and act.

Guidelines for Thinking

1. Perform creative visualization.

To overcome your built-in tendency to fear things, you need to cultivate an opposing frame of mind: one that is upbeat, confident, and easy to recapture whenever you feel yourself becoming anxious. I developed the following anti-worry visualization for this purpose. You can use it to overcome specific procrastination crises, but it's also good to practice it on a regular basis (for example, once a week) so that you can become increasingly more comfortable doing it.

Before trying it for the first time, study it until you feel you can recall the gist of it fairly well. Key words are italicized to help you do this. Then, perform it from memory at a slow, relaxed pace, hearing yourself mentally recite the directions, and giving yourself about a minute after each direction to savor the visual image you've created.

1. *Assume a comfortable position* somewhere that is quiet, dimly lit, and free from distractions. Some people prefer lying down with their legs straight and slightly apart, and their arms extended loosely at their sides. Others prefer to sit in a relaxed mode in a comfortable chair or couch.

2. *Close your eyes and take a few deep breaths* to relax your body—inhaling slowly through your nose, then exhaling slowly through your mouth. *Let go of any tension or tightness* in your body. *Allow the thoughts and cares of the day to drift away,* leaving your body light, your mind empty.

3. In this relaxed state, *picture yourself standing in the middle of a clearing in a densely wooded forest.* Imagine yourself slowly turning in a circle on this spot, looking at the edge of the clearing as you turn. Notice that there are very few gaps between the trees, and that you can't see very far into the forest.

4. Now, stand still again, and *feel yourself become totally motionless, as if you were paralyzed.* You want to

go forward into the forest, but your body refuses to move. You feel more and more strain. *Increase the muscular tension* in your arms, your body, your legs. *Let your anxiety level rise.*

5. Now, *imagine you hear a voice within the forest softly calling your name* over and over. As it continues to call, the *tension slowly drains from your body,* until it is all gone. You are still standing there, motionless, but now you are completely relaxed again.

6. Still relaxed and motionless, *hear the voice continuing to call your name,* gradually getting louder and louder. *You realize it is your own voice,* at its strongest and most beautiful. The voice stops and, then, several yards into the forest, *you see someone coming toward you.* You try to make out what this person looks like, but it's too shadowy to see well.

7. Still relaxed, imagine this shadowy figure slowly coming closer and closer to the clearing. When it's almost at the edge, *see that this figure is really you, only looking much more positive and self-confident* than you normally look. Notice what specific ways you look more self-confident.

8. *See your "new self" walk into the clearing and come to a stop in front of you.* Imagine yourself completely comfortable standing face-to-face with your new self. Now, *imagine that you hear your self-confident self say,* "You can handle much more than you think you can. Have more trust in yourself. You can move out of your comfort zone and take a risk. I'll be there to catch you if you fall, and show you the way if you get lost."

9. *Take these words into your heart.* Savor the hope and encouragement that they give you. Feel confidence building in your body, like a warmth spreading from your heart. Then, *imagine yourself slowly walking forward into the forest,* all the while sensing the more confident you walking behind.

10. Imagine that as you walk through the forest, *the trees become farther and farther apart, letting more and more sun shine through.* Finally *you come to a big meadow*—the end of the forest. *You look up into the clear blue sky,* filled with pride and contentment. Stay with this feeling as long as you wish, then *slowly open your eyes.* Notice how relaxed and calm you are.

2. When you put off making decisions about your assignments, daily schedule, or long-range academic goals, recognize that you ARE indirectly making a decision—to do nothing.

When you put off doing things, don't tell yourself it's because you can't decide what to do. Instead, recognize the truth: You *are* making a decision—to do nothing.

Doing nothing may be okay, at least for the time being. Sometimes it may be an appropriate decision: for example, if you need to wait for applications to arrive before you can apply for financial aid, or if you want to talk with your advisor and several key teachers before choosing your major.

However, it's likely that not making a decision may simply be a way of procrastinating due to self-doubt or fear of taking a risk. In such cases, putting off decision making may make things worse, as you put yourself at the mercy of fate, limit your options, and risk not achieving what you really want.

3. When confronting a challenge, acknowledge that it makes you nervous, but focus more on what could be exciting about it and what opportunities it could bring.

Remember, there's a thin line between being nervous or being excited about an upcoming event. As a worrier procrastinator, you're in the habit of leaning toward the nervous side of the line. To counteract this tendency, try leaning the other way.

Whenever you catch yourself thinking about the scary aspects of a new assignment or responsibility, shift mental gears and start focusing on what's exciting, stimulating, or inspiring about it. The more you do this, the more you'll develop an optimistic approach to your student life, one in which you give less attention to your fears, more attention to your hopes.

Also, never forget the value of a job well done. As you confront each new assignment or responsibility, periodically remind yourself exactly why it's worth doing in a timely and efficient manner. This affirmative activity will help you develop a greater desire to accomplish and a stronger belief in yourself.

As a worrier procrastinator, you need to reprogram yourself to look at the positive side of a situation not the negative one. Luckily, this training not only *does* good, but also *feels* good!

4. Although some assignments or other aspects of student life may intimidate you, guard against mentally "catastrophizing" them, or making them bigger and more threatening than they are.

No matter how tough a task may look, don't immediately assume that it's impossible for you to do it. Avoid starting out from an "Ohmygod!" orientation. Learn to regard student challenges as essential elements of your life. Yes, they'll require time, work, and perhaps assistance from others, but who said being a student was going to be easy? If it were, the experience wouldn't be very valuable to you as a person, nor would your degree be worth much in the outside world. Keep reminding yourself that you're in school to work hard and to grow from managing new experiences and learning new skills. You *can* do it!

5. Practice being your own best friend by believing in your skills, intelligence, and intuition and relying on them even when you have doubts.

As a worrier procrastinator, you're inclined to turn to other people—directly or indirectly—for help, comfort, or distraction whenever things seem troublesome. In effect, you're saying, "I can't do this all by myself." Such a statement lowers both your self-esteem and the regard other people have for your competence. Consequently, you continue to build an ever more fragile future for yourself.

Friends should be there to encourage and support you, but you also need to take charge of your own responsibilities. Excessive reliance on others creates worrisome dependency deep inside. Self-reliance creates inner strength.

Before you take your troubles to someone else, try taking them on yourself. Listen to the self-nurturing part of your personality that says, "I *can* do this!" Going over the facts of the matter, one by one, ask yourself, "What are my options? What are my preferences? What personal talents and strengths can I apply here? What resources can I tap?" If you wind up fumbling a certain task, be as kind to yourself as you would be to someone else. For example, if you get a lower grade than you wanted or aimed for, don't call yourself an idiot. Instead, take a sober look at what went wrong, and learn from your mistakes. Cultivating your inner resources instead of under-using them or ignoring them builds your self-confidence and helps you collaborate more productively with others, if and when such collaboration is necessary.

6. Follow a two-part process with a big decision (like going for an MBA): First, commit yourself to it ("I AM going to get my MBA"); then figure out HOW you're going to do it.

When you truly commit yourself to a goal first, the "how" part is far less likely to plague you. It's helpful to follow this two-part process with many decisions, but it's especially important to do so with a major one.

For example, if you are not fully committed to getting an MBA but only headed in that direction, you can easily be overwhelmed and thrown off course by all its implications: more years in school, higher expenses, greater competition, and more demanding courses. On the other hand, if you begin by seriously committing to the goal, you will find a way to achieve it. The path may be circuitous and filled with obstacles, but if your intention is clear, it will help you to manage whatever difficulties may arise.

Guidelines for Speaking

1. Avoid the use of qualifiers in your speech, because it tends to increase your indecisiveness and procrastination.

Qualifiers are words and expressions like "maybe," "perhaps," "sort of," "kind of," "try to," "practically," and "as much as I can." When you use them, you are making your statements tentative. Instead of dodging a firm commitment, speak more directly and affirmatively. Don't say, for example, "I'll try to get it done." Express more self-confidence by saying, "I *will* get it done." Instead of saying, "I'll read as much as I can today," be more assertive and say, "I'll read fifty pages today."

2. Replace simple "I can't . . ." statements, which weaken your resolve, with compound "I can't . . . but I can . . ." statements, which strengthen it.

By ending your sentence on an upbeat note, you direct your attention and that of your listener away from what you *can't* do and toward what you *can* do.

For instance, rather than complaining to a friend, "I can't complete the paper by Saturday," say "I *can't* complete the paper by Saturday, but I *can* finish my outline and make the charts." Rather than saying, "I can't afford to upgrade my computer now," say, "I *can't* afford to upgrade my computer now, but I *can* afford a new software program."

3. Instead of just asking a rhetorical "what if?" question, which will make you more apprehensive, go on to answer the question with a plan, which will increase your sense of competence.

As a worrier procrastinator, you can easily get into the self-defeating habit of using "what if?" statements to catastrophize situations and excuse your inactivity. Suppose, for example, that you continue to put off seeing your advisor about summer internships by complaining, "What if I can't afford to live on what an internship pays?" If you let this statement hang in the air, you not only increase your own blind anxiety about the future, but also influence your listener to agree with your fear and hesitancy.

Why not give yourself and your listener a break by answering your own question as positively as you can? Say, for example, "If the internship pays poorly, I'll have to budget my money better now so I can afford it" or "I'll have to discuss stipends for internships when I talk with my advisor."

4. Instead of just saying "I don't know," which fuels your self-doubt, add "but one thing I do know is . . . ," which builds your self-confidence.

The expression "I don't know . . ." (as in "I don't know how I'm going to do this assignment") is uttered by worrier procrastinators to short-circuit any deeper, more serious assessment of the situation. They say these words because it's easier than defining the underlying fears they have, or considering any action that has a potential for being—or going—wrong.

Rather than automatically saying "I don't know" in your own conversations and leaving it at that, make an effort to say something more specific by adding: "but one thing I *do* know is. . . ." For example, instead of merely complaining, "I don't know how I'm going to do this assignment," you might end on a more positive, action-oriented note by saying, "but one thing I *do* know is that I will ask my roommate how she's handling it," or "but one thing I *do* know is that I will get some more information from the library." Making a more definitive statement gives you something to start working with. Just saying "I don't know" leaves you stranded.

5. Rather than making a simple "I'm waiting . . ." statement, which encourages passive worrying, go one step further and make a "meanwhile, I'm doing . . ." statement, which fosters productivity.

Worrier procrastinators typically use "waiting statements" to buy time for procrastinating. "I'm waiting to see how I did on the midterm." "I'm waiting for the books to come in to the library." "I'm waiting until the weekend to begin this paper."

Don't let waiting statements pass by without adding a "meanwhile I'm doing" statement. "I'm waiting to see how I did on the midterm. Meanwhile I'm developing some possible extra-credit ideas." "I'm waiting for the books to be returned to the library. Meanwhile, I'm studying my notes." "I'm waiting until the weekend to begin this paper. Meanwhile I'm getting my other homework out of the way." Adding a "meanwhile I'm doing" statement means speaking of yourself as a doer instead of just a victim of circumstances.

Guidelines for Acting

1. Break down a large, intimidating project, such as writing a term paper or taking an exam, into a series of smaller, less threatening tasks.

As a worrier procrastinator, you're inclined to scare yourself into passivity by always looking at the big picture. It's much better to divide the big picture into small ones that are individually easier and more comfortable to consider.

Follow this three-part process:

1. Determine a specific date by which you want to have the whole project completed.

2. List all the small steps that are involved in that project.

3. Don't overwhelm yourself by tackling all the steps at once. Focus on one, two, or three steps at a time. When you've completed those steps, you'll be able to go on to the next ones in a more confident way, until you've completed all of them by your predetermined deadline.

For example, suppose you have to compose a professional-looking résumé. You might break that intimidating task into a number of less daunting ones: compiling a list of your previous jobs (paid and volunteer); writing descriptions of your skills; consulting books on writing résumés; making several rough drafts of a résumé, based on your research; showing your rough drafts to other people whose opinions you respect; and producing the final copy. As you do each small task, you'll become more and more empowered and encouraged to do the next one. Always bear in mind this truth: Doing creates the ability to do more!

2. To inspire yourself to be more productive and self-confident, read motivational books, listen to inspiring music, and collect encouraging quotes.

Prepare yourself well to be your own best cheerleader whenever you're tempted to procrastinate. Check out bookstores and Web sites for positive things to say to yourself during times when you're especially indecisive or stuck. Shop for motivational posters, audiotapes, and music to rev yourself up when you're feeling anxious or discouraged.

I often recommend that worrier procrastinators read Dr.

Seuss's book *Oh, the Places You'll Go* (N.Y.: Random House, 1990). It addresses with humor and optimism the obstacles and impediments that keep worrier procrastinators so stuck. It also provides just the right phrases to help readers move beyond their sticking points in a rhyming language that's easy and fun to recall.

Dr. Seuss (in reality Dr. Theodore Geisel) wrote the book for kids, but, like many children's books, it can be wonderfully motivating for people of all ages. During difficult times you can use such books to "re-parent" yourself with positive messages you may not have received in childhood. In doing so you can help heal your "inner child," who may still be needy, insecure, and confused.

3. Increase the time you spend with optimistic, self-reliant friends as you decrease the time you spend with pessimistic, complaining ones.

It's usually best if you start to think through a challenging new task or responsibility *by yourself* before turning to others for answers, opinions, or ideas. When and if it does come time to consult with others, it's much better to choose people who are generally optimistic, encouraging, and hopeful. Stay away from those who are generally pessimistic, discouraging, and cynical. They are likely to bring you down, get you involved in a "pity party," or make you dependent on them.

With these ideas in mind take a closer look at the people you know as well as new ones you meet. Invest more of your time with friends who encourage you to do your best, letting their confidence and enthusiasm rub off on you.

4. To avoid always being behind, attack one task every day that you've been putting off for a while.

Teach yourself the habit of *not* procrastinating by handling at least one long-postponed task each day. In addition to catching up on unfinished business, you'll also be guaranteeing yourself less pressure and more freedom to operate when unexpected assignments come along.

The task you choose shouldn't be a big, complicated, or fearsome one. It should be something small but significant—like deleting old computer files, phoning someone you've been meaning to call for months, or finally putting your most important research notes on file cards. You might even do something you really enjoy but haven't done for weeks, like ride your bike or write a poem. One of the main points of this activity is to be able to say to yourself, "I did it!" so you have the experience of how good it feels to get something completed and out of the way.

5. Take on a task every week that's constructive in itself, but that you're generally uncomfortable doing or even actively dislike.

Worrier procrastinators often stop themselves from doing something they need to do because they're not comfortable with it. In these situations they should tell themselves, "So what if I'm not comfortable with it? Comfort doesn't have to be my primary concern. The path of growth is riddled with discomfort. Do it anyway!"

Make a list of all the things you don't like doing, or are scared to do, or don't feel you can do very well. Consider *any* kind of activity that falls into one of these categories: for example, reading an article on statistics, driving at night, talking with your father, cleaning out the refrigerator, eating at a restaurant by yourself, balancing your checkbook. Then, every week do at least one thing on your list *on your own initiative,* that is, without someone or something else causing you to do it.

It may help to do this kind of activity impulsively as soon as you feel in the mood to experiment, rather than giving it much thought ahead of time. That way you're less likely to talk yourself out of it.

For example, suppose talking with instructors about course material you don't understand is on your list of things you hate to do. One afternoon, when you've got some free time, you may find yourself passing such an instructor's office. Thinking about this guideline, you might say to yourself, "What the heck, I'll drop in and ask my questions!" Now *that's* the spirit!

5

The Crisis-Maker Procrastinator

". . . BUT I like doing things at the last minute!"

Do you often say to yourself, or anyone listening, "I work best under pressure?" It's the motto of crisis-maker procrastinators. Some proclaim it proudly, intimating that they have special pressure-release capabilities that other people don't. Indeed, crisis-maker procrastinators in general tend to be quick thinking as well as compellingly dramatic. Others utter the motto more sheepishly. They realize that any skill they have in coping with an emergency is not so much a special ability as a necessary evil caused by creating the crisis in the first place.

The problem for both kinds of crisis-maker procrastinators—the proud and the sheepish—is that the pattern they've developed for themselves is not a healthy one. No matter how well they justify the way they function, the unhappy truth is that they're addicted to the adrenaline rush of doing things at the latest possible moment. Until they get that rush they have difficulty focusing on a task and are easily seduced into dropping it when a more enjoyable alternative presents itself.

Crisis-maker procrastinators are used to letting urgent

conditions or highly persuasive friends make their decisions for them. Their lives resemble a roller-coaster ride: First, they sit back and allow things to escalate, then they're suddenly jerked into the scary but stimulating highs of adventure, only to fall immediately afterward into the depressing lows of exhaustion.

They tell themselves they can't control this pattern, and, indeed, they wind up making sure they can't. They've become too dependent on the rush that comes from things getting out of control. Crisis-driven response has evolved into an essential element in the way they operate. As long as they're addicted to this pattern, it keeps them baffled about what to shrug off and what to attend to; what is honestly worth doing, and what is nothing but a waste of time. Always either passive or caught up in a frenzy, they lose perspective about their priorities.

Wayne, a nineteen-year-old college sophomore, often boasts about his crisis-maker procrastination. He sees himself as a hero, gathering all his resources at the last minute to study for an exam or pull together a term paper. He likes the challenge of doing things in the least possible amount of time, and it affects every area of his life.

For example, if Wayne needs to drive across town to meet friends for dinner, he waits as long as he thinks he can to set out in his car, gambling that all the traffic lights will be green and that he will find a good parking spot right in front of the restaurant. "I play a game with myself," he says. "Either I get there in record time, which is what I really want to do, or I've blown it. It makes life more interesting."

Of course, one reason why Wayne feels the need to perform such stunts to make his life more interesting is that he spends so much of his time dawdling around. He tells himself that he wants to accomplish things as swiftly as possible, yet paradoxically he wastes huge blocks of time until he actually gets started.

Wayne claims he gets too bored trying to manage tasks more responsibly or efficiently. Comparing himself to his better-organized girlfriend, he insists, "I admire her, but I could never be like her. Her way is too tedious for me. I get distracted too easily. Even when I assign myself deadlines, I usually don't keep them. I'll set the alarm, determined to get up early so I can make class or meet a friend, but then the alarm goes off, and I can't make myself get up. It's so much easier to go back to sleep."

Wayne believes he suffers from a lack of willpower. This may be so, but the deeper, underlying problem is crisis-maker procrastination. He's learned *not* to be self-motivating, but, instead, to let the heat of an emergency—or of an exasperated friend, lover, family member, or teacher—do the job for him.

Lori, a twenty-one-year-old junior, has developed a similar pattern, but she's not as boastful about it as Wayne is. Instead, she's usually down on herself, knowing how often her procrastination has resulted in poor grades, lost opportunities, and frustrated relationships.

Lori comes from an alcoholic family and as a result feels that she has never had control over her life. She sees herself as a scatterbrained person doomed to be out of sync with the world around her. She can't help putting off, ignoring, or even totally forgetting assignments until the last minute. Inevitably she then becomes hysterical about them, running around frantically to get them done right away.

"I know I don't plan things well," Lori admits. "I wait and I wait and I wait to study for an exam until I don't have enough time to do an adequate job. When I'm finally down to the wire, I go nuts. I'm not only going crazy trying to study, but also blaming myself, and griping about the bummer situation I'm in."

Lori knows what she does, *but* she thinks that's the way she is and nothing can change her. It's not unusual for her to wait until the last minute to look for something to wear to a party, even if she's known about it for weeks. Describing one such occasion, she said, "I went frantically searching through my closet. I threw together one outfit, yanked it on, yanked it off, and went on to the next one. After ten minutes, my room looked like a bomb hit it. I felt like a wild woman. Finally I started screaming in frustration. My roommate came in to calm me down and told me, 'You're so used to having chaos in your life that you keep on stirring it up.' I think she's right!"

And indeed she is! But Lori herself is wrong to think that she can't change. She wasn't born a crisis-maker procrastinator, and she is capable of learning how to respond differently. However, instead of taking matters into her own hands *before* a major crisis develops, she's waiting for—and, therefore, inviting—such a crisis to occur first.

The stories of Wayne and Lori differ in some respects, but they both illustrate the on-again, off-again pattern of life that this type of procrastinator experiences: adrenaline-charged highs preceded and followed by lethargic lows. Let's review the basic characteristics that all people who fall into this category have in common:

1. **Crisis-maker procrastinators have to get excited about something BEFORE they act on it.**

Crisis-maker procrastinators depend upon the pressure of a crisis to jump-start themselves. This is especially true when they're dealing with something that they don't want to do, and let's face it, most school assignments are not fun. Putting something off until the last possible moment is one of the easiest and most effective ways of guaranteeing that a comparatively exciting crisis will occur.

When the crisis does occur, they jump into action, often *over*reacting with excessive energy and hyperactivity. Until that critical moment, they *under*react to their task load. Either they ignore their commitments, or they claim, illogically, that they have plenty of time to do them.

Wayne, for example, approaches his schoolwork as some sort of challenge or game. He can't see any point in putting in regular time studying or working on his papers before the deadline is hanging over him. Or so he tells himself. Lori simply doesn't let herself plan much. Instead, she counts on last-minute panic to provide the momentum to carry her through. This kind of pandemonium is inevitable in the way she lives, so she tells herself, why *not* wait?

2. Crisis-maker procrastinators get bored easily, and have little tolerance for what they see as the "dullness" of managing tasks more methodically.

Crisis-maker procrastinators have difficulty responding to daily demands in a thoughtful, practical, and efficient manner because their attention is geared toward an entirely different kind of stimulus: a *crisis* demand. Other calls for their time and energy go unheard, unseen, and unaddressed: If it's not a crisis, they reason, it's not something they need to do anything about right now. Going against this lifelong conditioning seems totally alien to them. Without any strong incentive to do so they bore themselves just thinking about it.

We see this characteristic in Wayne's insistence that he

could never be like his better-organized girlfriend. He's convinced that what works for her would simply be too boring for him, even though he's never given it a fair trial.

Lori also can't give up her crisis addiction to live a less frantic, less chaotic life, despite the fact that her turbulent existence makes her miserable. It's as if she's afraid that without one crisis after another she'd be left in that state of physical and emotional lethargy she hates so much. She doesn't really see that the two states—crisis and lethargy—are codependent, and that an entirely different state of well-balanced efficiency would be preferable to either one of them.

3. Crisis-maker procrastinators overdramatize situations so that they can be the focus of attention.

Many crisis-maker procrastinators are highly theatrical people. They perceive themselves, and want others to perceive them, as heroes leading tempestuous lives. Procrastination repeatedly gives them all the dramatic elements they require. It creates conflict: the hero vs. the near-impossible task. It builds suspense: Will the hero get the task done? When? How? And it guarantees a thrilling climax: a victory against all odds or a horrendous defeat.

Wayne represents the fully flamboyant hero. He deliberately courts disaster by procrastinating, not only as a way of making life more interesting to him, but also as a way of making him more interesting to his friends. We can imagine them sitting in that restaurant waiting for him to make his grand entrance and wondering, "Will he ever get here? Did something happen to him? Did he try for a last-minute dash once again?"

Lori is not trying to be a hero by procrastinating, but, in reality, it's become a way she routinely gets attention.

Consider, for example, the time she was trying on outfits for a party. She wound up crying out in frustration, a signal for her roommate to enter the scene. Her roommate not only calmed her down, but provided a summation of her performance!

4. Crisis-maker procrastinators attempt to prove themselves or affirm their identity by living on the edge.

Underneath the crisis-maker procrastinator's sensational theatrics often lie deep feelings of emptiness, worthlessness, and helplessness. To counteract these feelings, they crave attention and importance, seeking high drama in their lives. Repeatedly procrastinating is a simple way to stir up such drama. By putting themselves at risk this way, they hope to shock themselves not only into *doing something,* but also into *being someone*—not just another person, but the central figure in a crisis.

Wayne exhibits this characteristic in the way he waits to do anything until he has a chance to do it heroically— that is, in the fastest possible time it can be done. It's a big gamble, but it's the only way he knows to bring himself to life.

Lori suffers even more than Wayne from low self-esteem. Crises enable her to escape these disturbing feelings in a frenzy of self-display. She runs around, gets hysterical, screams for help. Far from being a hopeless nonentity with no control over her life, she's a self-declared "wild woman!"

Wayne and Lori both possess all four basic characteristics of a crisis-maker procrastinator, but individually they're on opposite ends of a spectrum: Wayne boasts about the title, while Lori's embarrassed if not ashamed about it. Let's examine the life of a crisis-maker procrastinator more fully by considering my former client Jerry, who falls somewhere in the middle of that spectrum.

Jerry: The Crisis-Maker Procrastinator

Right from the start of our relationship, Jerry, a twenty-one-year-old economics major, acknowledged that he had conflicting emotions about the way he managed—or mismanaged—his tasks and responsibilities. "Sometimes I really get off on waiting until the final moment to do things," he said during our first session. "I even have a name for myself, 'The Eleventh-Hour Specialist,' and I get a kick out of other people calling me that. But then I have days when I wonder what the hell I'm doing, why I let myself get into the same extreme do-or-die pressure scene time after time."

When I asked Jerry to describe more specifically how it felt to "get off" on last-minute activity, he said, "When I finally get around to writing a paper or cramming for an exam, it's exhilarating. I'm totally involved in what I'm doing, my work is flowing, and I feel absolutely competent. When I succeed in finishing the job this way, I'm triumphant! It's like a big wave of joy and relief coursing all through my body. I congratulate myself, 'Yes! You did it again! Mission accomplished!' "

I asked Jerry to talk more specifically about the feelings he had *before* he finally took action. "To be honest," he said, "I don't feel much of anything for a long time. I know I've got work to do, but I can't bring myself to care very much. I'm more interested in getting away with *not* doing it. That always seems like the better, more desirable alternative."

A major reason Jerry felt so excited when he finally did his work under pressure was because he felt so apathetic prior to that moment. This emotional seesaw in his life had been bothering him more and more in recent years. In fact, it was his primary motivator for seeking therapy. "Lately it's getting harder to swing into action when I finally have to," he told me. "What I used to think of as excitement is seeming more like a nerve-wracking ordeal. I'm more mindful of that right after I've pulled an all-nighter, when I'm thoroughly wiped out, and mad at myself for not having handled things better."

Jerry was also starting to face the fact that his pattern of avoiding or delaying tasks was costing him plenty. "It's not like I have a lot of fun doing other things," he confided. "I realize that it might be better to start doing what I need to do earlier, so that I'm not constantly responding to an emergency. I spent all last weekend furiously doing a research report that was due on Monday, something I could have been working on weeks before. After only an hour of working on it, I thought, 'This is actually interesting stuff. Why didn't I start sooner?' You know, I could have done so much better on that report if I had, plus I'm sure I would have enjoyed it more! Why *didn't* I do it earlier?"

In the same conversation, Jerry went on to answer his own question. "I don't like the philosophy of leading a structured life," he said. "I like spontaneity and freedom. I enjoy uncertainty. Too much studying is not worth it. If my friend studies every day and graduates with a 4.0 average, and I have a good time and graduate with a 3.1, so what? Chances are we'll both be in the same boat in a year or two."

At this stage in his life, however, Jerry was not so sure he was willing to gamble on his future anymore. His crisis-making procrastination was becoming far too risky for him to ignore or dismiss cavalierly.

Jerry was a senior in college at the time, but, thanks to his procrastinating habits, he had so many incompletes left over from his previous two quarters that he thought he might have to stay in school another year in order to graduate. He had also failed a course that he thought he should take over to improve his average. The F had not really been earned: It had come by default because he hadn't been able to stir himself in time to do the required paperwork for a withdrawal or an incomplete.

"Sometimes when I'm very late doing something I end up ignoring it altogether," Jerry told me. "There's a critical moment that passes by, and after that I can easily switch into that 'oh well, whatever' mode. It's a bit scary, isn't it? Intellectually I know I should be more concerned about not graduating this year, but I can't seem to get as worked up about it as I should be. It's like the motivation part is missing in my brain. Dad gets more upset about it than I do. He's giving me hell, and I guess that will sooner or later force me into doing something about finishing up."

Throughout Jerry's life, his concerned parents had always been there to worry for him and, often, to bail him out when he got into trouble because of his crisis-maker ways. As much as they'd tried to help him, however, they'd also inadvertently reinforced his bad habits. He was left to think that he didn't have to be responsible like his parents until he "grew up," sometime far away in the future.

"I confess, I was spoiled," Jerry laughed. "I was spoon-fed everything. I come from a traditional family. Dad worked long hours at the office. Mom worked hard as a homemaker. Seeing this, I vowed, 'I'm not going to work as hard as they do, at least not while I'm young. It's not worth it. I'm going to have as much fun as I can!' And fun to me, of course, was simply not working. I thought, 'When the stakes get higher, and I need to work, I'll change. But not now!' Well, now was always now, and later was always later."

During Jerry's high school years he was diagnosed with ADD—attention deficit disorder. Because of this, his mom was very willing to work with him to make sure he got his homework done. "Mom was very well organized," he recalled. "Well organized enough for the whole family! She'd sit me down at the dining-room table to do my homework and hover around until I was finished. Sometimes she'd even go to the library for me or clip stuff I could use from the newspaper so I felt all the more obligated to stay at that table like she wanted. I'd be chomping at the bit to get out of there and do something else, anything else, but I knew I couldn't until she was satisfied I'd done all I had to do. She'd keep telling me, 'Don't you see? If you do it now, you'll be free to do whatever you want later. It won't be hanging over you.' But I didn't see things that way. I wanted to make myself happy right then and there."

After Jerry left home for college his mother was no longer around to make him do his homework in a timely manner, and he could procrastinate as much as he wanted. Nevertheless, he always seemed to have someone around who would prod him into action when it was absolutely necessary. During the time he was my client, the prodder in his life was his girlfriend, Gina. "I couldn't make it if it weren't for Gina," Jerry declared. "She's constantly doing these little things to make life easier for me, like searching the Internet for material that may be helpful to me with one of my projects. She also knows how to force me into getting things done when I can't get started by myself. Sometimes it eats away at me that I depend on her so much, but she doesn't seem to mind."

Of course, Jerry wanted to believe that Gina didn't mind because he relied on her so heavily. Looking back on his history of relationships, however, he should have been questioning that assumption. "The longest I've ever had a girlfriend was a year," he said. "The same pattern repeats itself each time. Things go along fine for a while. Then suddenly there's a big, ugly fight. She's upset that she does more for me than I do for her, and I say I'll change, and I do. I change for a week or two. Then I go right back to the way I was. Finally comes the big battle when I promise once again that I'll change, and she says it's too late and walks out."

By examining this relationship scenario more closely, Jerry came to see in it the same procrastinating pattern that he used with his classroom assignments. He would repeatedly let things drift along until a crisis developed. He would then furiously get his act together (or try to) until the crisis passed and things could be left to drift along again. Sometimes, however, the crisis didn't just pass. Instead, it cost him something he valued—something he wouldn't have lost if he'd only been a little more aware of and responsive to what truly mattered to him.

Jerry's crisis-maker procrastination also had a negative effect on his more casual relationships. He once said to me, "I often regret not keeping in touch with the people I liked in high school, or the people I've met in college who've moved away. I put off writing, phoning, or e-mailing them, or even answering them when they contact me. Unless there's a crisis, nothing ever motivates me to act, and I wind up waiting so long that it becomes too embarrassing to do it at all. I know I've hurt people this way, and I've certainly lost out myself, but that's how it goes. If I don't have a deadline, some things never get done."

Jerry would even let small maintenance chores turn into crises before he got around to dealing with them. "I totally neglect my car," he told me, "until there's a real problem. Last week, for instance, I had to pull over when I noticed the motor was overheating. That's my normal signal the car needs oil! As usual, I had to go through a hassle to get it done. It's stupid, I know, to operate that way, but there again, I had to wait for a crisis to occur."

As for Jerry's academic career, his lifelong habit of crisis-maker procrastination was finally coming to a head. He doubted whether he could ever be successful without taking firm action to overcome that pattern. Although he acted nonchalant about it, he did want to graduate at the end of the year and even go on to get his MBA. To do the latter, he knew he had to study for the GMAT's. But every time he sat down at his desk to start, his mind began wandering so much he'd quit in twenty minutes. Often he'd smoke a joint or drink a beer to try to put himself back in the mood for studying, but usually he just became too tired to do anything. He knew he'd never make it at such a pace.

Midway through his therapy, Jerry became more aware of his predicament and more determined to do something about it. "My motivation to change is that life is getting tougher now," he said. "The time for change has finally come. I'm tired of living the same old way—it's lost its luster. I can see that if I don't modify my procrastination habits now, they're going to cause even more problems when I'm out of school."

Jerry's foresight was 20/20. Crisis-maker procrastination typically does evolve into a much bigger problem after college for two reasons. First, pulling an all-nighter to get something done gets harder as you get older, and you can't usually devote the next day to catching up on your sleep. Second, after college, you're invariably working with teams (your family, your work unit, your community group) rather than all by yourself. Thus, any bad work habits you've developed are going to have a negative effect not only on your performance, but also on *their* performance as well. This factor makes it all the more important for you to manage work effectively—and all the more difficult for you to scramble around at the last minute to make up for your earlier procrastination.

Jerry began his change process very simply and easily by correcting one of his most conspicuous bad habits—speaking in extreme terms. Crisis-maker procrastinators tend to describe things as being either "the greatest" or "the worst," "fantastic" or "terrible," "completely fascinating" or "totally dull." This dichotomy in the way they speak reflects and reinforces their extremist behavioral pattern of being either crisis-driven or sluggishly inactive. When expressing an opinion they use very intense words for dramatic effect instead of more specifically descriptive words for accuracy.

Jerry made a concerted effort not to exaggerate in his conversation and to use more temperate, illustrative language. For example, instead of saying, "Doing that term paper was the worst experience I've ever had," he said, "I worked harder on that paper than on any other one this year, and it took me much longer than I expected." Rather than calling a vacation spot "the most incredible place in the world," he described it as being "a great resort town with friendly people and exotic food."

Jerry also employed other easy-to-learn techniques to overcome his inclinations toward crisis-maker procrastination. You can use them, too, regardless of how complex your particular pattern may be.

How to Stop Being a Crisis-Maker Procrastinator

As a crisis-maker procrastinator yourself, you no doubt were able to identify personally with many aspects of Jerry's problems. It's vital to continue this process of self-awareness over the next few weeks by taking the following steps:

1. Recall at least two different occasions when you *thought some task might ultimately be valuable or pleasurable to do BUT you never got started* because the prospect of starting bored you. For each occasion, ask yourself these questions:

• Why, specifically, did it seem boring to me—in other words, what particular "start-up" activities, conditions, or situations seemed so terribly tedious?

• What were the consequences of my not even trying this particular endeavor or project? How might things have been different if I had started it and then carried it through to completion?

2. Recall at least two different times when you *finished doing some task, BUT wasted time or got it done late* because you waited until a crisis forced you to act. For each time, ask yourself:

• What, specifically, was the nature of the crisis, and how, specifically, did it arise?

• What specific steps could I have taken to avert the crisis?

• What were the consequences of my wasting time or finishing late? How did I feel? What effect did it have on my project? On my relationships?

In addition to doing this kind of self-assessment every now and then, you need to practice new, more effective ways of thinking, speaking, and acting. Experiment with *all* of the recommendations in each of the three following categories.

Guidelines for Thinking

1. Practice creative visualization.

Crisis-makers need to learn how to relax in a positive, refreshing manner. Because they've always been so caught up in their habitual self-defeating cycle of excitement and collapse, they don't know what it's like to experience genuine peace of mind until they consciously work at it. Then they discover how much energy and satisfaction there can be when life is not always in turmoil.

Creative visualization is an ideal tool for this kind of training. It's an active approach toward capturing the imagination and making it work *constructively* rather than *destructively.* The guided imagery that follows below is especially beneficial for crisis-maker procrastinators because it enables them to feel the difference between the "deadening" experience of sensory overload and the "enlivening" experience of sensory balance.

Before trying this visualization exercise on your own, read the directions all the way through several times until you feel that you can recall their general flow. Key words are italicized to help you do this. Then get into a comfortable position some place that is quiet, dimly lit, and free from disturbance.

As soon as you're comfortable, silently speak the directions to yourself as well as you can remember them. Go all the way through the exercise with a slow, relaxed pace, making sure to allow a minute or more of quiet visualization time between each instruction. The entire activity is meant to last about twenty minutes.

If you wish, you can record the directions word for word on an audiotape to replay whenever you want. While recording the directions, speak in a slow, soothing voice, allowing about a minute of silence between each instruction. Another option is to have someone read the directions to you, in the same relaxing manner as you go through the visualization.

1. *Close your eyes and take a few deep breaths* to clear your mind, inhaling slowly through your nose, then exhaling slowly through your mouth. Now, as you resume normal breathing, *imagine that you are standing in complete and silent darkness.* You can't see, hear, smell, touch, or taste anything. *Feel yourself getting nervous about what might happen next.*

2. Suddenly, *a light switches on. You find yourself standing in a room, surrounded by the people who are currently making demands on you.* You run from person to person. You see how upset each person is, and you hear each person insist that you do something. *Feel the tension increase in your body.*

3. With all this chaos swirling around you, you *see a light switch on the wall to your left. Imagine yourself turning the switch off* and being plunged, once again, into darkness and silence.

4. Now, *see something start to glow a few feet in front of you.* See it continue to glow in the darkness until *you realize it's a very comfortable chair.* Hear a gentle voice

saying, *"Sit down and relax. You are going to be soothed in all your five senses."* You sit down and relax. It is still dark all around the chair, but you trust what the voice has told you.

5. Still sitting comfortably in the darkness, *you hear entrancingly soft, sweet music.* It reminds you of bird songs and the bubbling of springtime streams. It's the most soothing music you have ever heard. As you continue listening, *you feel more and more peaceful.*

6. See the darkness around you start to lighten. *You see a beautiful meadow in front of you,* with colorful flowers, waving grasses, and small groves of trees. It's a bright sunny day. The blue sky has a few white clouds sailing across it, and it's the most peaceful sky you've ever seen. *The fresh air smells delightful. It also feels wonderful* as it lightly caresses your body.

7. Still relaxing, *feel yourself becoming hungry. Look to your right and notice a small table there, filled with some of your favorite foods* [name two or three specific foods]. You start eating these foods, and they taste more delicious than they ever have before. You savor each morsel until *your hunger is completely and delightfully satisfied.*

8. Continuing to relax in your chair, you *notice how all your senses—hearing, sight, smell, touch, and taste—feel alive.* Linger in your chair, enjoying this pleasant, all-over stimulation.

9. Now, continuing to enjoy your newly charged senses, hear that *gentle voice again, saying, "You can calmly face*

whatever you need to face, and you can take care of whatever you need to do. You will always be able to revitalize yourself and feel as alive as you do now."

10. *Continue to relax, taking comfort* in the words you've just heard. Then, whenever you're ready, *slowly open your eyes.*

2. Think about multiple reasons to do an assignment, rather than letting last-minute stress be your only significant motivator.

Stress is a natural and essential part of life. We usually think of it negatively as anxiety or tension. We tend to forget that it also has a positive dimension as excitement or stimulation.

Therefore, in overcoming crisis-maker procrastination, your goal is *not* to develop a negative attitude toward stress, or to avoid stress whenever you can. Instead, you need to cease depending *exclusively* on negative stress to motivate yourself into action, and begin relying more on positive goals or desires to serve the same purpose.

Start by developing a list of things that can motivate you other than stress. Here are some possibilities to consider whenever you're tempted to procrastinate on a task:

• How can I make doing the task more fun?

• How can doing it well improve my relationship with teachers, friends, family members, or others?

• How can doing it well make me more independent or free?

• How can doing it well educate me in an area that I care about?

• How can doing it well enhance my physical, emotional, or mental well-being?

• How can doing it well benefit me academically, financially, or materially?

• How can doing it well improve my reputation or personal sense of accomplishment?

• How can doing it well increase my interpersonal power, authority, or self-esteem?

• How can doing it well make me feel more secure or self-confident?

• How can doing it well help me further my own short-term and long-range goals?

3. Appreciate that you may not feel interested in doing an assignment until AFTER you start doing it.

Crisis-maker procrastinators tend to assume that a task isn't worth doing if the *prospect* of doing it fails to intrigue or excite them. In other words, they insist that an activity *lure* them into action. In so doing, they remain essentially passive, putting themselves at the mercy of whims, distractions, and, ultimately, emergencies. Instead of actively deciding for themselves what they want to accomplish (self-motivation), they shrug things off, submissively letting external factors or fleeting moods determine what they wind up doing.

As a crisis-maker procrastinator, you need to coach yourself into adopting a more active and upbeat frame of reference. Rather than telling yourself, for example, "A paper has to interest me before I can get really involved," switch the words, and therefore the idea, around by saying, "I have to get involved in a paper before it can really interest me."

4. When thinking about a project or obligation, focus at least as much on the facts (for example, "this is a required course") as you do on your feelings ("I don't like having to take it").

Being a crisis-make procrastinator, you put more emphasis on how you *feel* than how you *think* or what you *know*. Feelings are important, of course. But constantly allowing yourself to be controlled by your feelings is putting yourself at a huge disadvantage. To improve matters, you need to shift your focus away from your resistance toward doing a certain thing (a passive, feeling-oriented point of view that breeds procrastination) to how you can take control of doing it despite your feelings (an active, thought-oriented point of view that discourages procrastination).

When confronted with a particular task or responsibility that you're inclined to resist, avoid drifting from moment to moment on your "gut feelings." Don't coddle yourself by saying, "If I feel like it, I'll do it; if I don't, forget about it!" Instead, ask yourself the following, more constructive questions:

- What part of it *could* I do now, whether or not it might feel good?

- What is likely to happen if I don't take action now?

• How will I feel about the situation *next week* if I don't do something now?

• How will I feel *about myself* if I don't do something now?

By strengthening your thinking processes, rather than giving in so immediately to your feelings of the moment, you increase your ability to tolerate frustration. This is an important life skill that builds self-esteem and keeps you committed to accomplishing your goals.

In addition, you need to stop ignoring or discounting truths that you *know* for a fact in favor of assumptions that you *feel* might be true. For example, avoid saying to yourself, "Even though this paper is due on Wednesday [a fact], I doubt it will make a difference if I hand it in on Friday [an assumption]." Or "I see the gas gauge is almost on empty [a fact], but there's probably enough gas left to last another day [an assumption]."

5. Avoid manufacturing crises by thinking in extremist terms (for example, "I've got a zillion things to do!"); think in more realistic and specific terms ("I've got three papers to write and two exams to study for.")

Resist your built-in tendency to complicate or "catastrophize" each new task or responsibility by thinking in exaggerated terms, like, "There's a zillion other things I have to do before the end of the week," "It's impossible to do this assignment the way my professor wants me to," or "I absolutely can't cope with this right now." Instead, focus your mental efforts on clarifying and moderating the situation by asking yourself specific questions, like:

• What are the most important "other things" I have to do this week? Besides doing these "other things," what could I do to at least make a step toward meeting this new demand?

• What can I do to give myself some time and space to "see straight," so that I can figure out how to manage all my responsibilities more efficiently?

• What particular aspects of the new demand make it seem impossible? What aspects may, in fact, be possible? What can I do—or propose doing—to make this new demand more reasonable than it now appears to be?

• How can I make it possible to deal with the whole task right now? If I truly am not able to deal with it right now, what particular aspects can I handle right now, or how soon can I commit myself to dealing with it?

Guidelines for Speaking

1. Use more "thinking" words in conversations (for example, I'm PLANNING to study tonight"), as you cut down on the use of "feeling" words ("I'm DREADING having to study tonight").

Communicating what you *think* about something instead of just blurting out how you *feel* about it will help you respond to obligations more rationally and less emotionally so that your overall approach is more well-balanced. Rather than beginning statements with expressions like "I feel . . . ," substitute or add thinking-related expressions, like:

- I've determined . . .

- I've come to the conclusion that . . .

- Here's what I think about it:

- I've decided that . . .

- Reason tells me that . . .

When speaking about achievement-oriented issues, restrain your use of feeling-related words, like *love, hate, excited, upset, crazy, afraid, troubled.* Instead, consciously inject more thinking-related words, like *intend, plan, remember, organize, prepare, determine, conclude, figure on.*

2. To avoid dwelling on the negative or passive aspects of student life (like having to write about an assigned topic that doesn't interest you), resist characterizing yourself in conversations as incompetent, helpless, or victimized.

When you tell someone else that you're powerless or feel put-upon, you establish a belief system that sets you up as a helpless victim. It then becomes difficult for you to take charge of your own situation. For this reason alone, guard against uttering melodramatic, self-martyring statements such as, "I've completely screwed this up," "That's the worst news I could have had," or "Things are beyond my control." Instead, talk yourself and your listeners into a more positive, productive attitude by saying things like, "I've let things go, but I will get back on track now," or "I'm confused about how to do this, but I will figure out a way to deal with it."

3. In describing school-related events or tasks, don't use overly dramatic, polarized language that only reinforces your addiction to crises.

Crisis-maker procrastinators are inclined to describe experiences according to extreme degrees of arousal—from "hysterically funny" and "totally mind-blowing" at one extreme to "unbelievably dull" and "completely stupid" at the other. This tendency reflects their belief that something has to be intense one way or the other before it's worth paying attention to and, therefore, worth mentioning.

To counteract this self-sabotaging drive toward speaking in extremes, use words or phrases that are more temperate in feeling: words like "upbeat" and "entertaining" or "disappointing" and "shallow." The more you work at avoiding extremes in your speech, the less addicted you'll be to a crisis-related perspective on life's events.

4. When discussing a task you need to do (for example, applying for financial aid), focus on the positive aspects ("I can get money out of this!") rather than the negative ones ("It's so much work and red tape!")

Just as you need to avoid belittling yourself when you talk with others, you also need to avoid bad-mouthing your tasks and responsibilities. It may be tempting, and it may even be appropriate, but it's definitely not helpful!

In your conversations, guard against dwelling only on what's awful about a particular college assignment or how upset you are about a certain course requirement. Instead, spend more time discussing how you can make the assignment more interesting, or how you might go about meeting the requirement more comfortably. Soon you'll get to the point where you begin such conversations on a positive note, perhaps never needing to express the negative side at all.

Guidelines for Acting

1. Keep track in writing of repetitive crises in your life, such as pulling all-nighters to get a paper finished on time.

Start using a daily or weekly journal to record those occasions when:

1. a crisis arose *because* you procrastinated about doing something, or

2. you failed to address a potentially problematic situation that you'd previously noticed *until* it became a crisis.

Compose a few sentences about each incident, so that you can more easily and clearly recall it later when you re-read the entry. Include statements about *why* you procrastinated, *what triggered* the crisis itself, and *how* you responded.

After a month of keeping track, look back over what you've written. Identify each kind of crisis that took place more than once, and note it on a separate end-of-the-month page. This will give you a list of the crises you're most predisposed to creating and about which you need to be especially attentive.

2. Write action plans ahead of time to deal with important school-related matters instead of waiting for them to turn into crises.

Using the "crisis record" mentioned above (guideline 1) as well as your memories of other past crises (see the self-assessment exercise you did earlier in this chapter), make a written list of all the major crises in your life that tend to occur repeatedly because you procrastinate. For each crisis, write at least one positive action step you could take in the future to avoid the recurrence of that kind of crisis.

Suppose, for example, that one of your list items is "being surprised that a paper is due earlier than I thought it was." Your action step might be: "Keep a calendar of due dates that I review at the beginning of each day."

Once you've finished your list, keep it handy. That way, you can refer to it often and monitor how well each of your action plans is working.

3. If you're a fun-loving or competitive person, invent a game or reward that can help motivate you to do an undesirable task.

Assuming you've got a playful nature—and many crisis-maker procrastinators do—why not capitalize on it instead of repeatedly letting it cause you trouble? When you're faced with a school-related assignment that you find boring, add some *constructive* excitement to the mix by creating your own game or contest for getting it done in a timely manner. For example, try to beat a set time deadline, organize dry study material into your own offbeat test questions, or create a clever mnemonic or memory aid for a list you need to memorize (like using the word *homes* to remember the Great Lakes: *H*uron, *O*ntario, *M*ichigan, *E*rie, and *S*uperior).

Also, think of an appropriate reward to give yourself afterward for a job well done. It could be a special purchase, like a CD, shirt, or piece of sports equipment, or it could be an exceptional indulgence, like a great meal out or a full-body massage.

4. To offset your need to stimulate yourself through crisis making, get your adrenaline flowing with activities that are more appropriately fun or competitive, such as sports, dancing, or performing in front of an audience.

Be sure to do many things on a regular basis that are athletic, exciting, or daring, so that you can get the same sort of physical and emotional rush that you're used to receiving from crises. Climb a mountain, play a competitive game of tennis, go jam on your guitar, or rave the night away. The more you get your kicks from these stimulating kinds of activities, the less you'll be driven to seek them from last-minute crisis management.

6

The Defier Procrastinator

"...BUT why should I do it?"

If you're a defier procrastinator, you're probably inclined to be independent, strong-willed, and dominant. Great! These are essentially positive attributes. Your negative ones, however, such as resenting assignments, ignoring obligations, and resisting authority figures may be causing you more problems than you think.

When we picture what defiers are like, we're most likely to imagine people who are actively, visibly intimidating, with angry mouths barking out refusals, arms crossed militantly at the chest, clenched fists shaking in the air. Some defier procrastinators frequently do behave this way.

Other defier procrastinators, however, present different, even opposite images: smiling mouths voicing agreement or open arms suggesting full cooperation. Often they create more burdens and difficulties than their more obviously combatant counterparts, because their defiance is well hidden beneath a guise of compliance.

In psychological terms, we say that the latter kind of defiers exhibit *passive-aggressive* behavior. They say they will accomplish a particular task, or meet a certain deadline, but then make little or no effort to do so. And why does this happen time and time again? Whether they realize it or not, it's because they resented the demand that was placed upon them and never really intended to do what they said they would.

Procrastination is a tool for passive-aggressive defiers, just as it is for overtly defiant ones. Both kinds of people use it as a means of getting their own way for as long as they can. However, because passive-aggressive procrastination can be so much harder to identify, it's worth describing in more detail before we go any further.

Passive aggression is a way of life that begins when a child first starts acquiring serious responsibilities: completing assigned chores, doing homework, meeting people at specific times. Instead of openly rebelling by saying no to something of this nature, the inwardly resistant child develops a pattern of saying yes simply for the sake of momentary appeasement, but then does not follow through. "I'll clean my room in a minute, Ma," says the passive-aggressive kid, who then puts the whole unwanted task out of his or her mind. Later, when the child is accused of not doing anything, he or she may passively deny the accusation and even defy the evidence by adamantly proclaiming something like, "But Mom, my room *is* clean!"

Passive-aggressive behavior is a form of indirect opposition that seems to work well until others eventually realize that they are being ignored, belittled, manipulated, or betrayed. In the course of time, this pattern tends not only to get its perpetrators into far more trouble than they anticipated, but it sabotages their relationships so that in the end they're left feeling mystified, misunderstood, and bewildered about what went wrong.

Passive-aggressive people have developed a pattern of responding in an evasive manner in order to prevent their being easily pinned down. If someone accuses them of not calling when they said they would, they reflexively offer such excuses as: "There were no phones around," "I did call, but the line was busy," "I didn't say I'd call, I only said I *might* call," or even "I forgot" when they didn't forget at all. When others express their annoyance, they dodge responsibility by saying something like, "Aw, come on! Are you going to get angry about *this*?" implying that the other person is at fault for being upset over something so trivial.

Nobody likes taking orders, but part of growing up is learning to negotiate and compromise with authority. However, passive-aggressive defiers, like more actively aggressive ones, can never quite bring themselves to do this. Both kinds of defiers refuse to be accountable for their failure to do what others expect them to do. But passive-aggressive defiers are more liable to delude themselves into believing that they accommodate others to some degree, just because they initially present an agreeable, cooperative front. They're also more prone to cast themselves as innocent victims—stuck in traffic, boring classes, dead-end jobs, and screwed-up relationships through no real fault of their own, when, in fact, their stubborn need to do things their own way is often a major contributing factor.

Whether or not individual defiers are actively or passively aggressive, their signature complaint is, "I could do it, BUT why should I do it?" What they mean when they make this statement varies according to the situation. Sometimes they're questioning the importance of the task at hand: ". . . BUT why *should* I do it?" Other times, they're implying that the task is an unfair imposition: ". . . BUT why should *I* do it?"

Either way, the message is one of dissension. Defier procrastinators in general are inclined to consider any outside demand on their time and energy as a threat to their individuality. Openly or covertly, they respond to that threat with indignation and resentment, followed by procrastination.

Shelley, a twenty-year-old junior, is an example of an *actively* aggressive defier procrastinator. She knows that she has a reputation on campus as a bitch, but she doesn't let it bother her, at least on the surface. She prides herself on being a fiercely independent person who doesn't need—or want—anyone to tell her what to do. She often resorts to fighting words in her conversations with others, as well as in her solitary outbursts: "How could he give this paper a crummy grade like B-minus!" "She doesn't know what she's talking about!" "I can't believe he's torturing me with that ridiculous assignment!" "Does she think I don't have anything better to do with my time?" She also frequently commits petty acts of token defiance, like returning her library books late or ignoring due dates for essays.

Having come from a family in which her mother was, as Shelley puts it, a "doormat" and her father dominated every aspect of each family member's life, Shelley became determined at a very young age that she was not going to be used by others or get trapped in anyone else's notions of what she should or should not do. However, she has not made any concerted effort to discipline herself to get tasks accomplished. Instead, she throws all her energy into being annoyed, resistant, and rebellious.

Shelley's defiance also makes it hard for her to sustain meaningful relationships. Friendships progress reasonably well as long as she gets to call the shots, but when others start asserting their rights or, even worse, holding her accountable for things, she gets verbally abusive and drives them off. Rather than appreciating these people as possible helpers or even just fellow students, she can't help seeing them as controllers who threaten her personal freedom to do as she pleases.

Shelley's not happy with her life the way it is. Too often her procrastination results in poor grades and unfulfilled dreams. From time to time she realizes deep down that she's her own worst enemy, but as she goes about her day to day life, she can't help getting caught up in fighting others whom she categorizes as foes.

Now that we've met Shelley, the self-avowed firebrand, let's look at the more common, but less obvious, type of defier procrastinator: the passive-aggressive one. Joe is a twenty-four-year-old third-year law student who wants to be viewed by others as a nice guy. He typically says, "Yeah, no problem," when he's asked to do something; but in the course of time he winds up making that task far more problematic than it needs to be by working on it too slowly, too sporadically, or too halfheartedly—and occasionally even dodging it altogether.

Joe was an only child who was raised as a latchkey kid by a very strict mother. He had to follow a rigorous schedule and do his homework and chores on time or she would scream at him for hours. He knew she was being unreasonable, but he had no way out: It was preferable for him to do things her way, whether he liked it or not, than to incur her disfavor.

When he entered high school, Joe began a form of silent rebellion. He would immediately say yes to whatever she requested, but then go ahead and do whatever he pleased. This kind of behavior kept him in the power seat. No matter how angry his mother would get about his failure to live up to his word, there was nothing much she could do about it. Her tirades had lost their power to intimidate him into action. Regrettably, he began behaving the same way with his teachers and other authority figures—always presenting a false front of earnest cooperation, but rarely living up to it. More and more he boosted his ego by outmaneuvering his obligations rather than by meeting them.

Now that Joe's in law school, he wishes he could change his habit of passive-aggressive procrastination, but he doesn't know how to go about it. He still feels defiant against anybody who tells him what to do, and too often that feeling determines the rebellious ways he thinks, speaks, and acts. He admits that he often gets a rush out of giving in to this feeling: "When I'm annoyed at a professor for giving an assignment I don't like, I deliberately avoid working on it for as long as I can get away with it. It's how I get even, or how I *think* I get even."

After graduating from college, Joe was so insecure during his first year of law school that he applied himself to his homework with uncharacteristic diligence. He did well, but unfortunately this success only convinced him that he could safely resume his pattern of cooperating as little as possible. Accordingly he got lower grades in his second year, and is now doing even worse in his third year. He's smart and aware enough to appreciate that he needs to tackle his procrastination problem *now* before he sacrifices his law degree, or, later on, his law career.

In examining the portraits of Shelley and Joe, we have seen significant contrasts between the two major forms of defier procrastination—active and passive-aggressive. Now, here is a summary of the characteristics that *all* defier procrastinators tend to exhibit:

1. **In order to appear more cooperative, defier procrastinators often avoid expressing their hostility directly and instead communicate it indirectly through procrastination.**

This pattern is most prevalent among passive-aggressive defiers, but it also exists among active defiers. After all, even the most belligerent person can't always say exactly how irate he or she feels. Sometimes the opportunity for speaking directly doesn't present itself. Other times, it would be too obviously self-damaging to do so. Procrastination offers a subtle, nonviolent, nonverbal form of protest: a means of saying "I won't do it" with action— or, rather, *lack* of action.

Shelley, for example, avoids screaming at her teachers when she's upset. For all her bluster, she's not that self-destructive! Instead, she rages *about* them to herself or her friends and then expresses her resentment toward her teachers by not doing the work they assign in a timely manner. She can't bring herself to perform as they expect, because that would imply servile obedience, so she deliberately rebels. Sadly, the only real victim of her rebellion is herself.

Being more passive than Shelley in nature, Joe depends even more heavily on procrastination as an indirect means of expressing his hostility. He claims to get a rush from it, and it's small wonder! Procrastination is the only course of action that gives him the sensation he's really doing something to assert his individuality. It's just too bad that his idea of doing something is, in fact, doing nothing.

2. Defier procrastinators consistently view life in terms of what others expect or require them to do, rather than in terms of what they themselves genuinely want or need to do.

Defier procrastinators are always on the lookout for an opponent. They're predisposed to avoid, resist, or fight against doing any tasks that someone else (dubbed "the opponent") imposes upon them. This defensive attitude keeps them focused on other people rather than on themselves. Therefore, they have only a vague sense of what, specifically, would bring them happiness or improve the quality of their life. All many of them can say is, "I just want everyone to leave me alone and let me do my own thing." Ironically, they're the ones who are having difficulty defining their own thing. And they're the ones who are viewing others as adversaries rather than allies who might help them reach their goals.

Defier procrastinators don't stop to consider that many of the tasks they resent are things they need to do not for *others* but for *themselves* in order to achieve their own personal happiness and success. They may even enjoy doing these allegedly unfair tasks if only they'd give themselves a fair chance.

We see this overall characteristic in the ways both Shelley and Joe feel dissatisfied with their lives, but can't really identify what would make them happy. They've decided that the source of their problem lies *outside* themselves, in the demands that others make upon them. In fact, their problem lies *inside* in their exaggerated reaction to requirements and demands and in their failure to take clear, responsible action on their own behalf.

3. Defier procrastinators automatically resent authority figures, and procrastination is their way of challenging authority.

Defier immediately get angry whenever they think that another person—or society as a whole—is telling them what to do. They interpret it as a threat to their own self-importance and individuality.

Defiers wouldn't feel so vulnerable to such a threat if they had more awareness of their own goals. Unfortunately, they rarely understand this dynamic. Usually all they can see is that they're being pressured and that their self-esteem somehow demands that they fight back.

In some cases, defier procrastinators view their behavior as a private battle against boring conformity. Thus Shelley refuses to return her library books on time and, as an act of subversion, will shoplift when items are, in her opinion, outrageously overpriced. Joe sees his defiance in a more mischievous, less militant light: He realizes that he puts on a facade of compliance with authority figures, but he describes this act of deception as playing a game, rather than waging a war.

4. **Defier procrastinators resist doing the kind of constructive self-examination that might enable them to see their problems more clearly.**

Defier procrastinators are very quick to read offenses into the motives and behaviors of others, but very slow to recognize how little they evaluate their own selves and how much they actually depend upon outside help. Time and again their own tendency toward procrastination keeps them from taking stock of themselves and forces the people who care about them to assume the thankless roles of overseers, servants, comforters, or saviors.

Defier procrastinators don't want to acknowledge this distressing state of affairs because it would be too humiliating for them. Whenever another person in their lives confronts them about it, no matter how lovingly, wisely, or justifiably, they fight back. It's what they've learned to do, even when it's not in their own best interests. So Shelley drives off her friends the minute they cease to be totally submissive while Joe has developed a defensive, mechanical "yes-saying" style that deflects his giving serious attention to anything unpleasant that's asked of him.

5. **Defier procrastinators tend to be pessimistic, which makes them less inclined to do things in a timely, effective manner.**

Because they always feel imposed upon by others, defier procrastinators regard life in general as unfair. This point of view gives them a perfect right to rebel and a perfect rationale for procrastination.

Shelley, for example, is not happy with her life. She can't help lashing out at anyone or anything that she perceives as making matters even worse than they already are. She also can't resist giving herself permission to avoid tasks that she's found contemptible, especially if it means thwarting the expectations of a controlling authority.

Joe also takes a negative approach to day-to-day life that reinforces his defier procrastination. As a child, he developed adversarial feelings about his relationship with his mother and his teachers that made him constantly expect the worst from them. He therefore had a legitimate excuse to procrastinate on the tasks they gave him, and little motivation toward better self-management. Now in law school, his lifelong inclination toward pessimism and procrastination is becoming so intolerable and so potentially ruinous that he's finally ready to do something about it.

Let's get a better idea of how all these characteristics function in the life of a typical defier procrastinator by examining the case of someone who is often passive agressive, but also openly defiant in certain situations. Matthew, a twenty-two-year-old first-year graduate student, is this kind of defier procrastinator.

Matthew: The Defier Procrastinator

When I first asked Matthew to tell me about himself, he described a person who seemed very productive. He was studying for his master's degree in communication, working part-time as an advertising sales rep for a radio station, learning the guitar, and playing on a city league soccer team.

It soon became apparent that Matthew was seldom as active as his schedule implied or warranted. If he was busy with anything, it was building up defiance. In fact, he was probably expending more mental and emotional energy resisting his obligations than it would actually take to meet them.

Matthew was well aware that his lifelong habit of dodging his responsibilities was finally catching up with him. "Now that I have a much fuller life," he told me, "I can see that I'm not going to be successful unless I change the way I do things—and even more important, the way I think about things."

As a graduate student, Matthew had more independence to set his own deadlines than he'd had as an undergraduate, but he also had bigger and more complicated assignments. He knew that this combination could ultimately spell disaster for him if he remained a defier procrastinator. He said, "Intellectually I realize that I now have to take my schoolwork more seriously and use my time and energy more wisely than I have in the past. But whenever I feel the least bit pressured, I get this overwhelming urge just to get out of what I have to do. This means somehow finding fault with it or blaming my situation on someone else, and then escaping with a supposedly free conscience. I know it's a quick fix, but I'm so used to operating this way that I can't resist."

Matthew's habitual procrastination almost kept him from getting his bachelor's degree when he did. During his last semester as a senior, one of his professors was set to fail him because he had missed over half the classes. As a retort to his professor, Matthew threw himself into studying really hard for the final exam and managed to earn a high grade—high enough that the professor agreed to pass him with a C. It was a squeaky finish that might have been a warning signal to someone else, but Matthew took it as yet more proof that he could get away with defying his teachers and the odds.

Matthew's rebelliousness met its Waterloo early in graduate school. As usual, he was polite and agreeable with his teachers and advisors on the surface. To them, he initially seemed like the model student, consenting to whatever they said. By the end of the first semester, however, they were well aware of his procrastinating tricks and his academic record showed it: He had two incompletes and one C out of five courses.

"If it weren't for my girlfriend at the time, I would have done even worse," Matthew admitted. "She at least badgered me into applying for the incompletes." Now Matthew was having to work twice as hard in school to make up the incompletes and keep up with his new course load. And he no longer had his proven helpmate: He had snapped back at her once too often for telling him what to do, even though his behavior kept crying out for such advice.

Matthew's part-time job was also teaching him that it was high time to overcome his defier procrastination. All his life he'd faced work with the same, secretly insubordinate attitude: "Why should I have to work so hard, especially if I can figure out ways not to!" As a result, he'd say "sure thing" to his bosses, while inwardly muttering "no way," and then go about applying the minimum amount of effort required to avoid being fired. He took pride in getting away with whatever he could, ignoring the stress it often caused him and the people around him. Now he had a job where he was essentially his own boss, free to set his own hours and objectives, and he didn't know how to handle it.

Seeking help with his job, Matthew attended a sales seminar on self-motivation soon after I first met him. At our next session, he reported, "They gave us a pep talk about having specific goals, then working toward meeting them. I don't recall ever thinking about my own personal goals. Instead, I've always thought about other people's expectations and how I shouldn't have to follow them."

Matthew was eventually able to see how his pattern of defier procrastination first became apparent in high school, when he'd occasionally refuse to do a specific assignment as an act of rebellion. "I hated when my friends automatically did what was expected," he said. "They were like sheep, no minds of their own, no backbones. I was an okay student, got good grades, ran track, played basketball. I made my parents proud. But just to spite them, I was always holding back a little—not turning papers in on time to get the higher grades they really deserved, or skipping as many practices as I could get away with, even though it meant not being as good as I actually wanted to be. Now it looks to me as if I was a rebel without a cause, but back then it looked as if I was really kicking butt."

Matthew's quarrel with his parents emanated from his belief that resisting authority figures was the best way to develop a stronger sense of self. He said, "It really bugged me that my mother and father never saw me as an individual seeking my own identity, trying to do things my own way. They would only see me as their eldest son, the crown prince, who was supposed to succeed and be a status symbol for them. So I'd always screw things up a little just to feel that I was in control, that I had a life they couldn't touch."

Matthew was especially resistant with his mother, who typically saw right through his superficially compliant, easygoing manner. "She'd nag me over and over again before I'd finally get around to doing what I said I'd do. I used to hate that nagging. It would only make me feel more resistant. I thought I'd lose my identity if I caved into her. I saw that happen to my father. He's a wimp, a defeated man, without a mind of his own. He'd say stuff like, 'Do what your mother wants you to,' 'Listen to your mother,' 'Check with your mother first.' I couldn't stand that!"

When Matthew started college, his habit of defier procrastination intensified dramatically. "I started hanging around with party animals," he recalled. "Courses seemed so boring and tedious. I wondered, 'How are they helping me *now*? They don't teach me anything that relates to me or my life.' I wanted something that would satisfy me immediately, and that meant having a good time. I told myself I deserved it. I also told myself I could change once I got out of college."

All through college, Matthew procrastinated in virtually every course, regardless of how easy or difficult it was. He'd skip classes for no good reason—simply for the hell of it. He'd avoid doing the reading assignments until an exam loomed, and then he'd only skim them. His papers were always thrown together at the last minute or later, assuming he could talk the teacher into an extension. His procrastination was a form of self-assertion that he didn't want to give up, no matter how much he himself suffered the strain of it. The only exceptions were classes where he liked the teacher well enough to want to earn his or her respect, and these classes were all too rare.

"I felt resentful toward most of my college teachers right from the beginning," Matthew remembered. "I got annoyed that they couldn't, wouldn't, or didn't understand where I was coming from. But every now and then there was a teacher like Ms. Brown, my art history instructor. Even though I didn't know a damn thing about art and resented having to take required courses, Ms. Brown was so enthusiastic and knowledgable, and so interested in my own perceptions, that I wanted to do my best in her class."

Matthew also had personal relationships in which he wanted to do his best, but inevitably he failed. In the give and take of everyday life, he was too committed to being the taker for these relationships to survive very long. He finally came to see that his own anger and self-righteous indignation doomed these relationships: "If someone starts giving me a lecture, or complaining about what's wrong with me, or even telling me what they think I should do, I get really provoked. Suddenly that person is the one who's the problem. Not me—I'm the one under attack!"

Every one of Matthew's girlfriends had given him the same ultimatum: "Grow up! Stop being so childish!" Exploring these relationships with me, he realized that he had a tendency to cast his girlfriends into the role of his mother—the nagging shrew—which, of course, meant that he could justifiably be the rebellious child. "My relationships with women always seem to end up the same way," he told me. "My girlfriend complains that I'm not being responsive enough to her needs. She says I automatically put her requests at the bottom of my list. And she's right! Eventually she breaks off the relationship. Then I blame her for leaving and take out my hostility on everyone else!"

There were some areas of Matthew's current life where he responded more appropriately, without defiance or procrastination. He enjoyed playing guitar and practiced on a regular schedule that he'd set for himself, and appreciated his instructor. He also performed well as a member of his soccer team, attending almost all the practices and accepting the coaching in good spirits. Thanks to these experiences, he knew he was capable of functioning without procrastination. He just didn't know how to transfer this capability to other areas of his life.

Meanwhile, Matthew was using his desire to practice the guitar or play soccer as an excuse to avoid doing his work as a student or a sales rep: "Why shouldn't I do what I really like?" he'd say to himself, justifying his procrastination, "instead of what other people think I should do?"

Matthew's rebelliousness was also obvious in his driving habits. "I seem like a mild-mannered guy on the street," he said, "but when I get inside a car, watch out! Especially if I'm late! I drive fast and loose to get somewhere and curse everyone else who's driving. They're in *my* way! They're the bastards!"

Given the way Matthew drove, it was no surprise that he often parked defiantly when and where he shouldn't. As a result, he accumulated lots of parking tickets, which he characteristically ignored. "I think I'd rather go to jail than pay them," he bragged. "Besides, I don't think they'll ever catch up with me because I've got an out-of-state license."

Matthew once summed up his dilemma by saying, "There's always a certain grumbling going on inside my head. 'Why do I have to do it?' or 'Why doesn't some other person do it?' or 'Isn't there something better I could be doing?' Sometimes I just sit there and do nothing, which is boring as hell, rather than summon up the energy to do something I know I have to do."

Together, Matthew and I worked on a program to help him break through his habit of defier procrastination. One of the most effective things he did was to keep a journal of all the occasions when he found himself thinking defiantly. Through his journal entries, he gained a better appreciation of the specific thoughts or statements that fueled his anger and tendency to procrastinate—for example, "I can't believe she's assigned all these chapters to read in a week," "I'm not going to let him tell me what to do," and "Who does she think she is!"

How to Stop Being a Defier Procrastinator

Like Matthew, you can put yourself on the road to positive change by taking a closer, more honest look at how much you hurt yourself by procrastinating. Here's a self-assessment exercise to get you started:

1. Recall at least two different occasions when you were faced with a project or activity that you *wanted or needed to do BUT never did* out of defiance. For each occasion, ask yourself these questions:

   • Whom was I defying, and why?

   • What were the consequences to myself of not doing it?

   • What were the consequences to others?

2. Recall at least two different occasions when you *finished something BUT wasted time or got it done late* be-

cause you were caught up in defiance. For each occasion, ask yourself:

- Whom was I defying, and why?

- What were the consequences of my wasting time or being late? How did it make me feel? What effect did it have on my relationships?

To solve your own personal problems relating to defier procrastination, you first need to develop greater awareness of how they developed. Then you need to make some changes by practicing new, more empowered ways of thinking, speaking, and acting.

Guidelines for Thinking

1. Practice creative visualization.

When you create for yourself a richer, more invigorating inner life, you become less inclined to focus antagonistically on what other people expect of you. One of the best methods of doing this is to practice visualizing on a regular basis.

Initially you may have difficulty "seeing" clear images with your mind's eye as you follow the guidelines. If so, do the best you can to experience specific thoughts, shapes, colors, and sensations that seem appropriate. As you continue to practice, you'll be able to visualize more easily.

Creative visualization is a skill that's well worth the effort of building. By training your imagination to develop stronger mental pictures of who you are and what you want, you acquire more self-confidence, along with a greater feeling of aliveness. Thus you'll be much better equipped to deal with life in a positive, solution-oriented manner rather than a negative, complaining one.

The visualization exercise that follows is one that I created specifically to help defier procrastinators become more even-tempered and productive. First, read it all the way through several times, until you know the gist of it. You don't need to recall it word for word. Key words are italicized to help make the process easier for you.

When you feel you're ready, go ahead and try it out. Assume a comfortable position somewhere that is quiet and pleasant. Then, silently speak the guidelines to yourself as you recall them.

Go all the way through the activity in a slow, relaxed pace. Make sure to allow about a minute of quiet visualization time between each guideline. The whole exercise is meant to last about twenty minutes.

If you want, you can record the guidelines as printed (except for the words between brackets) on an audiotape. Then you can replay the tape whenever you want. As you make the recording, talk in a slow, soothing voice, allowing a minute of silence between each instruction. Another alternative is to have someone read the guidelines to you, in the same, relaxing manner, as you do the visualization.

1. *Close your eyes and take a few deep breaths* to relax your body, inhaling slowly through your nose, then exhaling slowly through your mouth. *Let go of any tension or tightness in your body. Allow the thoughts and cares of the day to drift away,* leaving your body light, your mind empty.

2. Beginning with your present age [state your age, e.g., twenty-two], *slowly count backwards three years at a time, pausing at each age to develop a few images* of what your life was like then [e.g., "twenty-two . . . nineteen . . . sixteen . . ."]; stop when you reach the last age

for which you have fairly clear memories [for most people, between the ages of five and eight].

3. *Remaining at this last age* [restate the last age mentioned], *imagine yourself doing something that you use to do, all on your own, that was pleasurable and empowering* [such as throwing a ball, singing, running, solving puzzles, making sand castles]. As you continue to perform this activity, notice how good it makes you feel about yourself, how energized you are.

4. Gradually *bring this activity to a conclusion, and allow yourself a few moments of pleasure* and pride in having done it.

5. Now, slowly *return to your present age. Imagine yourself choosing of your own free will to engage in an activity that brings you similarly positive feelings*—a fairly uncomplicated pursuit that you can complete in a moderate amount of time. You start to perform this activity, feeling good about what you're doing.

6. You continue doing this activity at a relaxed but steady pace, becoming increasingly more involved as you go along. *Imagine yourself gaining more and more satisfaction from it,* even if some parts of it may be routine or difficult.

7. Now, imagine yourself completing this activity. *After you've finished, pause a few moments and take pride* in what you've accomplished. Feel good that you set aside the time do this task and that you directed your energy toward it in such a rewarding way—without resentment or resistance. Savor the new energy and enthusiasm for

life that you're now experiencing, thanks to what you've done.

8. Now, *picture a specific task in your present life that you do not want to do, but that you realize needs to be done*—a task that also takes only a moderate amount of time. *Imagine that you have chosen to do this chore of your own free will, then go about doing it* in the same relaxed but steady way that you went about doing the previous activity.

9. Now, *see yourself finishing this activity and feeling good about what you've done.* Take pride in the fact that you chose to work on this project in your own way, and that you completed it without experiencing resentment or resistance.

10. Now, *hear a voice within you saying, "You can choose to do a job well, even if someone else gave you that job, because doing it well makes you feel good about yourself."* Pause a moment to realize the truth of these words, and, when you're ready, slowly open your eyes.

2. Think about school assignments as requirements of the course that *you're* choosing to take, rather than demands that others are imposing on you.

As a defier procrastinator, you have learned to view every request or expectation from the outside world as an assault on your right to remain an independent person. As a student, you naturally have lots of people telling you what to do. Remember, however, that you're in this position temporarily because you have chosen to be there in order to create a better future for yourself. Therefore, it's usually in

your best interests to be as cooperative with school author-
ities and systems as you can reasonably be. You don't need
to be an automaton. You can suggest changes in the assignments and procedures; but they'll never be adopted unless
you first express and negotiate them in a respectful manner
with the other people involved.

Student defier procrastinators typically find it difficult to
consider outside direction as anything other than a challenge to their independence. Their instant reaction is, "The
teacher's making an unfair demand, and I resent it!" For
your own success you need to learn to be less defensive
right from the start. Instead of immediately rousing yourself into rebellion whenever an authority figure asks or even
tells you to do something, try speaking to yourself more
temperately and rationally, like, "Okay, this is something
I'm expected to do. How shall I respond?"

3. Before reacting to something in anger, calm yourself down and start reasoning intelligently and practically about it.

Keep close watch on how you think and feel when you're
faced with an outside request, and identify signs that you
may be overreacting. For example, when you first en-
counter a demand, does your mind begin racing with reasons *not* to meet it? Do you mentally curse out the other
person and call the expectation unfair? Do you start envisioning ways to get out of it? Do you bang the table with
your fist? As soon as you recognize what your personal
danger signals are, you can keep yourself from falling into
your old pattern of defier procrastination and, instead,
move forward in a more effective and ultimately rewarding
direction.

4. Instead of just complaining about some school-related assignment, start generating multiple options for responding to it effectively.

As a general rule, defier procrastinators consider only three limited response options for every assignment:

1. *comply as requested,* (the "good student" syndrome), in which case they are viewed favorably but lose their own personal sense of individuality;

2. *defy in an active manner,* (the "bad student" syndrome), in which case they are viewed unfavorably but maintain their own personal sense of individuality; or

3. *defy in a passive-aggressive manner* (the "double message" syndrome), in which case they may be viewed favorably (although only for a short while) and at the same time maintain a certain amount of their own personal sense of individuality.

To overcome this very narrow way of thinking, you need to look at each newly assigned task as a unique situation that calls for the fullest possible range of *positive* response options. Each of the options you generate should be capable of satisfying at least some of the teacher's expectations as well as some of your own desires. You can then exercise your individuality by choosing the one particular option that you consider to be the best. This type of rational decision making is bound to be more productive and gratifying in the long run than blindly following through on one of the three "knee-jerk" options already outlined.

Let's suppose, for example, that your instructor has assigned you an especially difficult project to do as part of the course requirements. Without giving it much thought, you'll most probably do one of three defier-procrastinator things: (1) say nothing and begin the project, even though you loathe every minute of it; (2) say something angry to your instructor about his or her unfairness and balk at doing it as requested; or (3) agree to do it but privately decide that you'll get around to doing it in your own sweet time and in your own idiosyncratic way. Whichever one of these three options you pick, chances are extremely high that you won't do well on the project.

Think about how much easier, happier, and more productive your life would be if you could apply some constructive thought to such a situation *before* reflexively choosing one of those three problematic options. Here are just a few of the more positive response options you might develop for yourself:

• Think about the demands on your time and energy for the time period involved, determining (if possible) various ways that you may be able to do the project as requested. If it truly seems impossible, note the obstacles to doing the project so that you can discuss them with your instructor.

• Investigate with your instructor possible strategies for the upcoming project so that the project itself doesn't seem so intimidating and the instructor doesn't seem so cold or remote.

• Divide the project into separate, smaller tasks, such as doing the preliminary research, determining the methods you're going to use, completing the first phase of the assignment. Then, considering the time and resources available to you, figure out how you might go about getting each individual task accomplished most effectively.

• Review your other responsibilities for the time period involved, and plan constructive ways to shift responsibilities around so that you have more time for this project.

• Negotiate with other instructors who are expecting things from you to find out if there are any mutually satisfying solutions to the situation.

• Figure out several different more comfortable ways of doing the project than originally requested and submit them to your instructor for discussion.

Always be *specific* rather than *global* in your response to an outside demand. This means restraining your immediate tendency to overreact. By assessing each situation calmly and logically before you decide how to respond, you increase your control over what you eventually do. At the same time, you decrease the pressured feeling that you have to act according to someone else's rules.

5. Although defiance may sometimes be justifiable, choose your battles carefully, weighing what's most worth fighting for.

Defiance takes up a lot of psychic energy. Even when your get-even strategy is not to do anything, your mind may continue to obsess on a teacher, friend, or system as the tormentor and you as the victim.

Regardless of whether you can justify the accuracy of these images, they are very self-crippling ones to carry within your psyche. For this reason alone, it's a good policy to minimize defiance as much as possible. Reserve your acts of rebellion for truly life- or sanity-threatening situations, and hope these situations are few and far between. You may initially feel like a hero when you're defiant, but if you rebel too often or too long, you just end up feeling exhausted.

6. Cultivate an internal "nurturing parent" that can minimize your defiance while encouraging you to act in your own best interests.

Talking to yourself is a great idea, especially if you say encouraging words. Imagine that inside you there exists a nurturing parent who is your very best friend and teacher. This parent is not a critic, nor is he or she a sidekick whom you use to support your own worst impulses. Instead, he or she is a mentor who speaks with wisdom, maturity, and compassion, helping you to attend to tasks that you know deep down you need to do.

Invoke this inner nurturing parent in your interior dialogues by striving to be both caring and levelheaded, rather than purely emotional. When you're confronted with a challenge you are resisting, ask this part of you specific questions about how, where, what, why, when, and even whether to do it, instead of complaining about the whole task in some sweeping, exaggerated tirade.

The nurturing parent within you is a valuable resource that can help make things better for you, as long as you keep yourself open and honest in using it. When you get stuck in a self-destructive rut of defiance because you don't want to do a particular task, it's there to lift you out by reminding you of basic truths that you might otherwise over-look, such as:

• Not everything needs to feel good in order for you to do it.

• Something that feels good to you in the short term (like partying instead of studying) may turn out to be bad for you in the long term.

• Something that feels bad to you in the short term (like getting up early to hit the books) may turn out to be good for you in the long term.

Guidelines for Speaking

1. Instead of impulsively using words to blame or attack when you're upset, take time to think about the situation more rationally so you can express yourself more constructively.

As a defier procrastinator you need to train yourself not to be so quick to use confrontational words in response to un-wanted requests or feedback—words like, "You gave me an unfair grade!" "Get off my back!" "You're never satisfied!" "You expect too much from me!" For the moment, such words may make you feel powerful, but they don't resolve anything, and they only make the other person feel more defensive, hostile, and uncooperative.

As a start toward less pointlessly defiant speech, try making statements that begin with "I" instead of "you" when expressing negative feelings about a task or relationship—statements like, "I feel that my paper deserved a higher grade." "I get upset when you find fault with something that I think I've done pretty well." "I don't think you understand my point of view." When you talk about *your* feelings, and begin your statements with "I" instead of "you," the other person involved will generally be less defensive and more willing to listen.

2. When you make a verbal commitment, like "I'll be ready to give my report in two weeks," keep your word!

In taking on a new project or assignment, defier procrastinators often say what they think the other person wants to hear simply so that he or she will leave them alone. Later, they just refuse, forget, or neglect to live up to what they said.

Don't let this happen to you. Instead, be careful to state only what you really plan to do, then sincerely commit yourself to doing it. This approach is especially important when you're engaged in a group project and expected to do your fair share in a timely manner.

Later on, if you feel the need to change your plans, or if your plans go awry, take responsibility for the situation with a direct statement to the person or people involved. You might say, for example, "I know I told you I'd complete it by Friday, but I misjudged how much I had to do." If you can, suggest another, more certain deadline at the same time. And, once again, mean what you say!

3. If you haven't followed through on something you said you would do, admit it instead of trying to weasel your way out of it.

You're only inviting trouble by letting the other person assume that you're doing what you promised when, in fact,

you're not. Even if the other person never holds you accountable for procrastinating, you are developing a habit of
getting away with things that will eventually erode your
self-esteem and personal sense of accountability.

Whenever you haven't done something that you said you
would, let the other person know in a timely and honest
manner without making up an elaborate excuse or getting
defensive all over again. If an apology is in order, make it
simple, direct, and personal: for example, "I'm sorry *I*
haven't finished it yet." Above all, avoid an apology that's
designed to acquit you of any responsibility, like, "I'm
sorry that *you're* upset about this" or "I'm sorry *things* got
so out of hand."

Defier procrastinators understandably hate making apol-
ogies. To them, it's losing ground. It's as if they're admitting
they were wrong, stupid, lazy, or incompetent. In fact, their
dread of possibly having to apologize often explains their
extreme defensiveness. As a defier procrastinator, you need
to appreciate that an apology is a reaffirmation of your
own responsibility, a way of showing respect for the other
person, and, quite often, a first step toward renegotiating
terms.

When apologizing, do not go from one extreme, defiance, to the other, self-punishment: "I feel so awful!" "I'm
such a screw-up!" "I never do anything right!" Instead,
simply express your regret, and, if appropriate, add a
pledge toward some specific, positive action in the future:
"I'm sorry I didn't get this done by Friday. I'll have it for
you by Monday."

Also, don't let yourself get into too many situations when
an apology is, or might be, necessary. Repeatedly apologizing without doing any better the next time is part of the
passive-aggressive syndrome.

4. Speak more positively about school assignments instead of constantly talking about how much you resent them.

Making positive statements in your conversations, like, "it's a tough class but I'm learning a lot," helps motivate you toward constructive action. Making negative statements, such as "it's a tough class and there's too much reading," does just the opposite. It drains you of energy and predisposes you to procrastinate.

Eliminate the following overly defiant phrases—and others like them—from your speaking vocabulary: "Don't tell me . . . " "What gives you the right . . . " "How dare you . . . " "I'm not the one, you are . . . " "You can't expect me to . . . " Instead, try speaking in a way that's more even-tempered and open to cooperation. Always stay focused on the facts involved in the situation (for example, "I have a twenty-page term paper due before Thanksgiving"), not just the feelings or the personalities (for example, "I hate writing term papers" or "this teacher's a real slave driver").

5. Keep in mind that HOW you speak is as important as WHAT you say. Guard against a hostile tone of voice or antagonistic body language.

It's been said that 80 percent of communication is your tone of voice, your facial expression, and your nonverbal gestures, while only 20 percent is the words you use. For this reason it pays to be attentive to how you sound and look when you speak. No matter what specific words you say, your mode of speaking and bodily movements may portray you as hostile, exasperated, condescending, mean-spirited, or sarcastic. They may contradict your words, communicating a more belligerent or negative message than you mean.

To avoid any misunderstandings that may result from such mixed messages, make sure your vocal tone and body language match your words. If you convey cooperation with your words but your look or gestures indicate non-compliance, don't be surprised if what you actually say is taken the wrong way. Becoming more aware of how non-verbal expression affects your listener is an important step toward improving your ability to communicate.

Guidelines for Acting

1. When you tell others you'll do something, be sure to do it!

Always remember to give importance to what you've told others you'll do, even if it means writing it down and putting it in a highly visible place. Then make a direct commitment to live up to your words. The purpose of doing this is not to appease others but to build up your own self-respect and inner strength.

When you say yes to something but later change your mind, inform the other person as soon as possible, saying, for example, "I've had second thoughts about what I told you yesterday, and now I don't think I can finish the project by Wednesday." You can then propose an alternative solution, if it's appropriate. If some event suddenly comes up that keeps you from being able to meet your original deadline, you also need to let the other person know right away and, if appropriate, suggest a revised deadline: for example, "I've been sick this week and have fallen behind in our group project. How about having our discussion next Wednesday, after I get caught up?"

The important thing is to take every opportunity to do what you said you'd do. If you know you need to renegotiate tasks or time frames, then do so. The more you just let time pass by, the more you reinforce your overall tendency to procrastinate.

2. Instead of REACTING angrily to an assignment, strive to ACT constructively by taking control over it.

Be cooperative in your approach to any academic requirement. Aim toward deciding on a rational action, rather than reacting in a knee-jerk fashion by complaining and defying. The former strategy puts you in charge of the situation. The latter one gives the other person the upper hand.

For example, if you really don't think you can complete a term paper by its due date, given all your other assignments, ask your teacher if you can have more time. Your teacher may say yes or tell you to take an incomplete. Even if the answer is no, you will have acted in a straightforward manner, gaining your teacher's respect and bolstering your own self-esteem. It's far better than reacting in a muddled, potentially destructive manner by griping over the situation and doing nothing.

To remember this guideline more graphically, think of a powerful adult as opposed to a powerless child. In a task-related situation, an *adult* is a person who is wise enough to work out a plan giving him or her a voice and the freedom to function as an individual, while still considering other people's needs. A *child*, however, is a person who is comparatively naive and unskilled, and believes that his or her only options are to comply or defy. These images can help motivate you to behave more like a powerful adult, and less like a powerless child.

3. When engaged in a group project, strive toward working WITH the team, not AGAINST it.

Bear in mind that you are not living alone in this world. In many ways you *are* dependent upon other people for your success, well-being, and happiness. Therefore, you need to stay at least somewhat open and accommodating to what others may want.

Whether you're on campus with your teachers, classmates, or advisors, on the job with your supervisors, coworkers, or clients, or at home with your family or friends, you work best when you function as a team player, not as a rebel fighting everyone around you. Develop the habit of cooperating with others and supporting their efforts instead of attacking, obstructing, or rejecting them.

4. Because students have limited control over their obligations, satisfy your need to do things YOUR way by getting involved in specific pursuits that you can completely control.

Defying as a way of life offers a very limited and short-lived pleasure at best. To make matters worse, it almost always brings with it a certain amount of pain and trouble. You can get much more satisfaction out of doing something active and positive to express your power: a specific, constructive project that you can enjoy and completely control. Depending on your personal preferences, it may be writing a song, reorganizing a file system, running a marathon, or building bookshelves.

Make an effort to incorporate such projects into your ongoing life. You'll soon find out that the more you do on your own that feels productive, the less you need to defy others in order to satisfy your ego.

5. As a means of broadening your limited comply-or-defy perspective, take a course in assertiveness or conflict resolution to learn better negotiation skills.

Courses in assertiveness and conflict resolution help defiant people (as well as overly timid people) by teaching them to be more effective in an important life skill—negotiation. Specifically, these courses can teach you how to be more even-tempered and successful in expressing your concerns, eliciting information, clarifying misunderstandings, forging compromises, proposing changes, securing commitments, and motivating others to assist you. These capabilities will be useful to you far beyond your student life, as you continue to interact with authority figures, coworkers, friends, and family members.

7

The Overdoer Procrastinator

"... BUT I have so much to do!"

In every facet of life, our speed- and success-oriented culture pressures us to work faster, harder, and better. As a result, we often feel as if we're somehow running behind. It's an unfortunate situation for all of us, but it's particularly troublesome for students who are overdoer procrastinators. As basically industrious, self-reliant, and cooperative individuals faced with countless academic and social opportunities, they're already inclined to assume more responsibilities than they can handle, and cultural reinforcement of this bad habit only makes matters worse.

If you're an overdoer procrastinator, you probably say yes to things too easily and too often. As a result, you don't leave yourself enough time to manage your most important tasks. You also have difficulty relaxing—that is, taking a few hours to rest and recharge your energies. Instead, you get involved in yet another activity that perpetuates your busyness.

Sometimes you may work to please others—not simply to be kind but to gain approval and to make sure you're liked. Other times you may work to bolster your own sense of strength and self-sufficiency so that you won't be so bothered by an inner feeling of emptiness or guilt. Whatever your conscious or subconscious motives may be for involving yourself in particular activities, you always seem to be working too hard or too much because you're consistently shouldering an inappropriately large number of responsibilities.

Overdoer procrastinators typically don't give themselves the chance to learn from their mistakes or the freedom to make decisions in their own best interests. Because of their lifelong, automatic habit of saying yes to new tasks, they never acquire basic skills in decision making, prioritizing, time management, and assertiveness—all of which are essential requirements for academic success. Instead, they rely a lot on procrastination (their indirect way of saying no) to try to gain some control over their work overload.

The characteristic BUT factor for overdoer procrastinators is: "I'd like to get it done—BUT I have so much to do!" Unfortunately, they often use this statement as a justification for neglecting their responsibilities toward others and their obligations toward themselves. They're so caught up in day-to-day activities that they rarely get around to meeting their own personal goals or simply enjoying student life.

It can sometimes be difficult to identify students as overdoer procrastinators. Frequently they themselves don't realize that they're creating their own problems because they can so easily blame their difficulties on the high-pressured academic world. Also, from their personal point of view—and in the eyes of many observers—they may appear to be workaholics rather than procrastinators because they're always busy *doing* things.

In fact, students who are overdoer procrastinators take

on a dizzying array of tasks and consequently often neglect important ones. Some tasks they never start. Others they never finish. Many of the rest they rush through, completing poorly or way behind schedule. Over and over again they find themselves with too much on their plate. Eventually this situation leads to fatigue, burnout, and resentment that they work so much harder than other students yet don't seem to have much to show for it.

Let's trace this pattern in the life of Tara, a freshman in college. She illustrates what I call the "social" kind of overdoer procrastinator. Besides taking on too many tasks all on her own, she is easily talked into doing whatever her friends want her to do. Because she's a popular, outgoing person, this means constantly having a heavy work and social schedule that's out of her control.

Tara doesn't think of herself as an overdoer procrastinator, but she knows that she's got the problems we've just described. "I'm constantly frazzled," she says, "and I never seem to have time for myself. What drives me to work so hard is what *others* want, not what's good for me. I have no discipline, no personal priorities, no real sense of who I am. I have loads of friends, but inside I feel very lonely."

In addition to being out of touch with her own needs, Tara has difficulty identifying what she genuinely likes, apart from pleasing other people. "When I'm by myself," she complains, "I have a hard time doing anything. It's like I don't have a clue how to relax. So I work for hours but don't get much done, or I trance out in front of the TV or get involved in reading a magazine, and there goes the day. Sometimes I even get so anxious being alone that I go out looking for someone else, or someone else's chore to do."

Tara doesn't feel that she intentionally procrastinates. Instead she becomes so busy doing so many different things—

working on her school assignments, keeping up with family events, running errands for friends, doing volunteer jobs for campus organizations, and just plain partying—that she's rarely able to get any one thing completed in an effective, timely manner. Her schoolwork tends to suffer the most. She's repeatedly late with assignments, and she knows the work she turns in is not as organized as she'd like it to be.

Erik, a junior in college, is not as sociable as Tara, but he, too, is an overdoer procrastinator. Instead of giving in to people out of a desire to please them, he seeks to impress people that otherwise intimidate him. Therefore, like Tara, he assumes far too many responsibilities, only to remain overworked and underprepared to meet many of his deadlines, especially the academic ones.

Erik's pattern of overdoer procrastination began early in his life. "I've always been the strong one in my family," he states. "My father died when I was twelve, and I became the man of the house. I started working at fifteen to bring in extra money for the family. I developed a habit of being busy all the time and getting involved in things bigger than myself because I wanted people to admire my efforts. I know I'm doing too many things because I'm late, exhausted, and overwhelmed all the time. Clearly something's wrong!"

Now that Erik is in college, the pattern continues. As a member of the football team, he feels that he is doing something definitely worthwhile. Unlike most team members, however, he is also taking more courses than he needs and trying to stay active in more student organizations than he has time for. He also assumes more than his fair share of household work. "I have a roommate who hates doing stuff around the apartment," he says, "so I'm the one who usually cleans up, fixes things, shops, pays the bills, and talks with the landlord. If I complain to him about it, he just shrugs it off and asks, 'What are you so uptight about?' "

It certainly sounds as if Erik's roommate is imposing an unfair burden on him; but Erik acknowledges that he actually seeks that burden just to be in control and be the "strong one" of the team. As Erik says with a certain amount of pride, "I don't have many real friends, but I've got a lot of people who are dependent on me."

Although Erik thrives on busyness, that doesn't mean it's really good for him. "I don't know how to have fun," he admits, "or how to take it easy. I like football season because it's so incredibly busy I don't have to think about what to do. I just do it! We practice twenty hours a week, we have a game every weekend, plus workouts, travel, and pep rallies. And I've still got my full load of homework to do. But you know, it's strange. I get more schoolwork done during the season than I do afterward, when I have more time. It's not my best work, but it's usually finished right on time. I can't seem to apply myself in the same way when it's all up to me to get organized. During the football season, I've got no choice. Of course, even then, schoolwork's the last thing I get around to!"

The personalities of Tara and Erik differ in several major ways, but they both depict characteristics that all overdoer procrastinators share:

1. **Overdoer procrastinators have difficulty saying no to people or asking them for help.**

Many overdoer procrastinators think that saying no is being selfish. Actually, it may be far more self-serving to say yes just to earn approval from others.

It can be even harder for overdoer procrastinators to

ask for help. In their minds, to do so is an admission of weakness or an inability to be self-reliant. It also opens them up to possible rejection, which would be hard for them to tolerate.

As a result of their reluctance to decline, delegate, or ask for help with tasks, overdoer procrastinators are left with a huge amount of work to do all by themselves. It's small wonder that it often takes them an excessively long time to finish projects, and that they frequently fail to get certain tasks done at all.

For example, both Tara and Erik overschedule themselves because they don't say "no" to others, even though they realize they're already swamped with work. They also can't bring themselves to ask for assistance when it's clearly appropriate to do so. Tara is too sensitive about imposing possible burdens on others, while Erik is too keen on appearing strong and masterful.

2. Overdoer procrastinators tend to take on more work than they can reasonably manage in order to compensate for inner feelings of unworthiness.

Deep inside, overdoer procrastinators suffer feelings of emptiness and self-doubt. They believe that they need to work extremely hard in order to prove themselves or gain acceptance. Unfortunately, as much as they work, they never really believe they're doing enough or will be successful with all the tasks that they've committed themselves to. In fact, they often aren't—not because of their lack of talent, but because of the inordinate volume of work they're usually trying to handle at any one time.

Overdoer procrastinators can't shake the notion that their value is based on other people's opinions of what they do. As a result, they either don't develop a clear sense of their own personal needs, goals, and desires, or they give them very low priority. They also don't pay much attention to their own feelings until they feel completely burned out.

This lack of self-esteem is apparent in the way that Tara does whatever anyone else wants her to, and becomes anxious, bored, or bewildered when she's all by herself. We can also perceive it in the way that Erik enjoys having people depend upon him, but fundamentally feels uncomfortable depending only on himself.

3. Overdoer procrastinators lack self-discipline, especially in regard to personal needs and goals.

Instead of actively deciding for themselves what they're going to do and when and how they're going to do it, overdoer procrastinators passively leave it up to fate, relying mainly on whatever or whoever is staring them in the face at the moment. By keeping themselves so continuously busy, they avoid stopping long enough to plan a better, more efficient, and more reasonable work schedule. Proceeding as usual, they put off as much as they can for as long as they can, rather than coming to grips with the reality of their situation.

Unfortunately, the easiest things to put off without attracting attention or disturbing others are personal needs and goals. And so Tara, for example, has not taken the time to think about what *she* really wants out of life; and Erik feels the constant need to become involved in something larger than himself as a way of feeling important and worthwhile.

4. Overdoer procrastinators tend to assume so many different kinds of responsibilities that they get confused about priorities and find it hard to focus on individual tasks.

Throughout their college years, overdoer procrastinators suffer enough from the sheer *amount* of work they undertake. But to make matters worse, they also increase their problem by taking on too many *different kinds* of work. As hard as it is to prioritize tasks within one particular field of endeavor (such as determining which academic responsibilities are the most important), it becomes even more difficult to establish priorities among tasks in different fields (such as determining the relative importance of specific social, personal-growth, job, and relationship responsibilities balanced against specific academic ones).

Furthermore, trying to remain mindful of all these different tasks without the help of any predetermined priorities keeps overdoer procrastinators in a perpetual state of distraction. As a result, whatever or whoever screams the loudest gets the attention.

In general, overdoers commit themselves too heavily in too many different directions. With so many tasks confronting them wherever they turn, they simply throw themselves into *doing,* instead of thinking first about what's most important for them to do. This makes it easy for them to procrastinate on certain chores without realizing it or feeling overly guilty about it. After all, they're just too busy with other things!

Tara, for instance, stays heavily involved with her friends, family, and campus organizations to the detriment of her schoolwork. Clearly something has to give if she's going to do better academically. Erik also spreads himself too thin to do as well as he wants to do in his studies. He likes being busy on all fronts and believes he actually does more work this way, but it's not really *better* work. Like Tara, he too easily confuses more with better.

5. **Overdoer procrastinators have trouble relaxing and leading an enjoyable, well-balanced life.**

Overdoer procrastinators are only familiar with two extreme states of being: furiously busy or completely wiped out from having been furiously busy. Their self-image is based on work—they're either doing it or not doing it. They don't develop a richer sense of who they are, what they enjoy, and what they want out of life that can both underlie and transcend their role as "doers." This makes it very difficult for them to be by themselves, with nothing pressing to do.

Often overdoer procrastinators will say they wish they could just relax, but when the opportunity presents itself, they're somehow at a loss. Tara, for instance, never really enjoys downtime but trances out with TV or easy reading. She can't be comfortable simply being alone with herself because she always thinks of her value in terms of doing things with or for other people. Erik feels similarly barren inside. "I don't know how to have fun," he confesses. "I don't even know how to take it easy."

Now that we've heard from Tara and Erik, let's get even more closely acquainted with a former client of mine who was a typical overdoer procrastinator. Her name is Holly, and when I met with her, she was a twenty-five-year-old graduate student in education.

Holly: The Overdoer Procrastinator

When Holly came to me, she knew how inclined she was to procrastinate, and she'd already begun trying to break this bad habit. She was consulting me to learn more specifically *why* she procrastinated, *how* she could better anticipate problematic situations, and *how* she could prevent those situations or handle them as effectively as possible. "It took me seven years to finish college," she told me. "I don't want to spend another seven years getting my master's degree!"

Summing up her college years, Holly admitted that she'd always taken on too much and been scattered about managing her life, but she insisted that she'd never been what most people would call a time-waster. "I was very active all during college," she said. "I always had a full load of credits, plus I worked part-time in the library, sang in the chorus, and took part in every drama club production. And I was a member of student government for four years. One year I was even student body president. Sad to say, that was my *first* senior year!"

Holly admitted that her academic responsibilities suffered because of all her other activities. In effect, they were the last things she got around to fulfilling, when, by rights and by her own ambitions, they should have been the first. "I thought I was doing so well in college," she told me, "but now when I look back on it, I see I was really doing too much. I was proud of all the things I did, and my parents were, too. They would constantly brag about me to their friends. And so I fooled myself into thinking I was some sort of superachiever. But when it came down to the bottom line—the grades and credits I received at the end of each semester—I wasn't doing well at all!"

After five years in college, Holly, still a junior, could no longer avoid facing the truth about herself. For whatever reasons, her busyness was a way of putting off her academic work and, ultimately, her graduation. Some of the friends she'd made as a freshman had already been through graduate school and were now starting their careers. Feeling as if she were falling slowly but surely behind the times, she finally confronted her procrastinating behavior. "Enough is enough!" she declared. Sincerely wanting to get on with her life, she dropped most of her extracurricular activities, buckled down to her studies, and finished college over the next two years.

The Holly who came to my office was a more focused, self-determining person than the Holly of several years before. "Now I can't wait to get my master's and land a full-time job!" she exclaimed at our first meeting. "I want to prove to myself, my friends, and my family that I can do it! I so much regret starting my teaching career this late. I'm twenty-five years old, and I still haven't had my first real job. That's why I want to know more about procrastination and how to beat it. I don't want to create as many problems for myself in life as I did in college."

Our discussions of Holly's past revealed that she came from a family of procrastinators. "Both my parents talk a lot about what they're *going to* do," Holly said. "You believe them at first, because they sound so sincere, but it usually turns out that they don't do most of what they say they will. Mom's always dropping her own projects to help other people, and then complaining that she has no time for herself. And Dad's always saying he's too worn out by the weekend to do the things he promised he'd do."

Speaking about this habit her father had, Holly recalled, "It used to upset me a lot when I was a kid. He'd promise he'd take me somewhere I'd want to go, like a ball game or a movie. Then at the last minute he'd tell me he couldn't do it." Her disappointment over her father's reneging no doubt helped fuel her own desire not to disappoint others by saying no to them, however appropriate saying no might be.

Looking back at her high school days, she could see that she started procrastinating then in the same ways that both her parents did. She recalled, "A friend would say, 'Want to go to the mall with me?' and I'd say, 'Sure!' even though I'd promised myself I would organize my closet or study for an important test. Pleasing my friend would take precedence over everything else, certainly over what I needed to do for school. Afterward I'd be so zonked that I couldn't do anything that required thinking!"

Holly was particularly embarrassed now about the way she behaved with her high school boyfriend. "Whatever I thought would please him," she said, "I would do. I would even go to his house and clean his room for him. My friends would think I was crazy, but I figured, 'What's the big deal? I like to organize things, so I'll organize his stuff.' I know he needed it–he was a number-one slob!"

Holly's insights into her high school procrastination problems only came years later, when she realized that she'd never really resolved them. "I didn't see then that I was hurting myself by trying to do everything for friends I cared about. Trying to solve their troubles was only making my problems harder to manage. I'd get so busy that I'd crash, and then nothing got done, no matter how important it was!"

Throughout high school, Holly was inconsistent in her approach to her assignments, often putting them off for other pastimes until she finally had to throw herself into a last-minute frenzy of work to get them done. "I was always so easily distracted from doing what I had to do," she remembered. "A person asking me for a favor, or even just being there and seeming to need something, was so much more compelling to me than reading books or writing papers."

Holly's college career was not much different. It, too, was characterized by a great deal of energy with little focus or concentration. The result was a life that seemed to go in many different directions at once. Living this way made her slightly dizzy all the time, unable to see what was really happening to her, or to make constructive, day-to-day decisions about the best use of her time.

Holly's most vivid images of college revolved around what she did with and for other people, rather than what she did on her own (like her studies). When I once asked her to identify what she thought was her major problem in college, she said, "I could instantly be sidetracked by friends who popped into my dorm room or, later, my apartment. I'd have to be with them, and tuned into them, rather than doing whatever else I had to do."

Once she recognized this tendency Holly took measures to keep it under control. For the first time since she left home after high school, she was living with only one roommate—a woman with a full-time job—and the two of them had set a firm policy limiting the number of distracting visitors.

Holly was also taking better stock of herself and her life. "I realize I don't have to be a superperson and do everything," she said. "I'd like to get more involved with what's important to me and actually do something worthwhile instead of a lot of nonsense activities that have little real value. I want to do better in the future than I have in the past."

One of Holly's strongest desires was to define more clearly her long-range personal goals, so that she could be more responsive to them instead of whatever seemed to pop up. One particular goal that she'd always cherished, but hadn't done much about, was to become proficient at oil painting.

A year before we met, Holly had finally started painting in earnest, but she wasn't working at it the way she wanted to. "I enjoy it very much," she told me, "but I persist in starting new paintings without ever finishing them. I've now got a dozen or more half-done sketches leaning against the wall of my bedroom. I should either complete a whole painting, or not even begin it! It takes so much out of me to have so many loose ends hanging around. I keep getting enticed by the new painting and letting go of the old one that's still in progress. But then it haunts me that I'm not accomplishing what I set out to do!"

Meanwhile, Holly was continuing to have some of the same old difficulties she'd always had completing her school assignments in a timely fashion. "I would give anything to complete my course requirements on schedule," she sighed, "but, frankly, it's still hard for me to stay on track. It's so much easier just to grab at the nearest, or most interesting thing to do."

Holly was, in fact, doing better with her graduate courses than she did in college, but she knew she had to do better still to realize her ambitions. "I have to teach myself how to set priorities and then stick to them," she declared. "Believe me, it's an uphill battle! I no longer feel such a strong need to please people, and I'm not always putting my own needs on hold, but I still get distracted too easily."

Holly was hopeful that graduate school would finally provide the incentive to change that had somehow evaded her during college. "It's easier for me to apply myself to my studies now because I know I want to get my master's degree and become a teacher. In college, I didn't have such a clear idea of why I was there, or why I needed to know what was assigned. In graduate school, it's a more well-defined matter of becoming skilled in your chosen field, then going out and getting a good job in that field. I'm also more financially independent now than I was in college, so I take my time and money more seriously."

Holly's tendencies to procrastinate in graduate school

also seemed somehow more reasonable, acceptable, and, therefore, manageable than her similar tendencies in high school and college. "When I procrastinate now," she said, "it's actually more legitimate. What I mean by that is that I'm busy doing things that are truly important, like working part-time jobs and going to school. Now when I say I don't have time, I really don't! Before when I said that, it wasn't altogether true—I could have had more time then if I'd stopped doing so many trivial things. I still do procrastinate, and I still need to learn how to use my time more effectively, but I don't think I'm nearly as clueless as I was back then!"

Being an overdoer procrastinator, Holly needed not only to manage her responsibilities more efficiently, but also to engage in leisure activities that were more pleasurable and restorative. Only then would she discover the most productive ways of pacing her time and energy.

Like Holly, you can learn to break free from your pattern of overdoing and procrastinating and take better charge of your life. Begin by practicing the following, more constructive ways of thinking, speaking, and acting.

How to Stop Being an Overdoer Procrastinator

If you scored high on the "overdoer" part of the quiz earlier in this book, then your story probably has many similarities to Holly's. Now it's time for you to take a closer look at that story so that you can identify some of the specific patterns that sap your personal time and energy. Here's a self-assessment activity to get you started:

1. Recall at least two different occasions when you *finished projects, BUT spent too much time doing them or*

got them done late because you did much more than you needed to do. For each occasion, ask yourself these questions:

• Why, specifically, did I do much more than I needed to? What were the consequences of spending too much time doing it, or of being late? How did I feel? What effects did it have on my grades? On my relationships? On my life?

2. Recall at least two different occasions when you *wanted to do something important, BUT never got around to it* because you were too busy doing other things. For each occasion, ask yourself:

• What other things, specifically, kept me from doing that important matter? How significant *to me* was each "other thing" I did, compared to that important matter?

• What were the consequences of not getting that important matter done? How did I feel? What effect did it have on my grades? On my relationships? On my life?

Continue reviewing your past periodically in order to develop a better understanding of how overdoer procrastination has influenced your life. Also, start following each of the guidelines for thinking, speaking, and acting that appear below. As you read through them now, keep reminding yourself that time and energy are limited and precious resources. When you squander them, there's not much time left over to accomplish your goals.

Guidelines for Thinking

1. Practice creative visualization.

Overdoer procrastinators find it hard to relax because they assume that relaxation means "doing nothing"—the opposite of their typical "do everything at once" working style. In fact, relaxation does something vitally important: It enables you to release tension so that you can restore the personal energy that's been depleted by so much overdoing.

When you relax, your mind can still be active in a playful, invigorating manner. This is especially true when you engage in creative visualization. With repeated practice you can develop the skill of relaxing your mind in all sorts of creative and energizing ways that you yourself devise.

I created the visualization exercise that appears below especially for overdoer procrastinators. It encourages you to let your mind *rise above* problems to a more constructive state of peacefulness. Overdoer procrastinators need to make this kind of mental shift from time to time to help themselves cope more effectively with their workload.

Before doing this visualization, read all the guidelines carefully several times until you can recall them fairly well. It is *not* necessary to memorize the guidelines word for word. Key phrases are italicized to assist you in this effort.

When you're ready to go ahead, assume a comfortable position somewhere that's quiet and free from distraction. Then, silently recite each guideline to yourself as best you can. Go through the imagery in a slow, relaxed pace, allowing a minute or so of visualization time between guidelines. The entire exercise is intended to last about twenty minutes, with lots of built-in time to envision and relish individual images.

If you want, you can record the guidelines on an

audiotape and replay them whenever you want. While you're recording them, speak in a slow, soothing voice, and leave about a minute of silence between each instruction. You can also have someone else read the guidelines to you in the same relaxing manner as you do the visualization.

1. *Close your eyes and take a few deep breaths* to relax your body, inhaling slowly through your nose, then exhaling slowly through your mouth. *Allow the thoughts and cares of the day to drift away,* leaving your body light, your mind as empty as possible.

2. Now, imagine *you are walking along a path through a wooded area.* You don't really know where you are, but you're content to keep walking for a while until you find a place where you can rest and get your bearings.

3. You continue walking along the path, farther and farther, until *you come to a V-shaped fork,* where the path splits into two. Both paths look the same, and you don't know which one to take. Not wanting to waste time, *you proceed down one of them,* but you still keep feeling uncertain and rushed.

4. *You continue to walk down this path, noticing that the trees are getting closer together.* You worry that you're going deeper into the woods and won't find a place to stay. *You come to a crossroads:* one path on your left, another on your right, and a third straight ahead. All three paths look the same, and you don't know which one to take. Not wanting to waste time, *you proceed down one of them,* but you still keep feeling uncertain and rushed.

5. You keep on walking. *You turn a bend, and there are trees in front of you, but no path.* You turn around, and *you can't see the path anywhere!* You realize that you are truly lost among all these trees. *Feel the tension rise in your body* as you realize this.

6. Now, *tell yourself that you're going to calm down,* that you're going to stop and think for a moment. *Feel yourself lean your back against a tree and relax your mind and body.*

7. As you rest against the tree, *you gaze into the woods* and *you notice there's a tower* directly ahead. *You walk over to the tower and see steps* leading to the top. *You climb these steps to the very top* of the tower.

8. Now at the peak of the tower, *you can see clearly over the surrounding treetops.* Look all around, and notice that there are many other towers just like this one scattered throughout the woods. Looking directly ahead of you, *see a river a short distance away, going from your left to your right, with a path running along its near bank.* Notice that *the path to the right ends at a nice, cozy inn* with a "Welcome" sign out front. *Feel relieved* at what you see.

9. Now, *climb back down the tower* and walk into the woods toward that river you saw. *You come to the river and see the path* running along it. Feeling confident that you know where to go, *turn right, and follow the path to the inn* you saw.

10. *You enter the inn and see a comfortable chair* waiting for you in the front room. *You sink down into this chair,* heave a sigh of relief, and relax. *You close your*

eyes and hear a sweet voice saying, "You always have the power to take charge of your life and to see what needs to be done. Simply rise above where you are and take a good look at where you want to go." Enjoy the pride and peace of mind that these words bring you and, when you're ready, *open your eyes.*

2. Think of the student experience as not only hard work, but also as an adventure.

Don't stay caught up in the "overdoing" grind! Keep reminding yourself that there's a lot more to student life than work. Ask yourself, "What changes do I need to make so I can look back on these years as both educational *and* enjoyable?" Why not make some of those changes *now?*

Periodically take a good, hard look at your daily activities and ask yourself, "How fulfilling are they? What's missing? What's being neglected?" Your answers may indicate that you need to spend more time and energy on what *you* really *want* to do (both now and in the long term), as well as on what you're required to do in your courses or what your friends want you to do.

3. Remind yourself that going to school means having to make choices.

You need to admit to yourself that no one, not even you, can have it all—top grades, a great job, a hot love life, intense involvement with your friends, strong family connections, an active sports life, and lots of good-time activities all at the same time. You have to make day-by-day choices about the best uses of your time and energy. As you do this, you also need to be careful not to neglect any one aspect of your life for too long!

Besides admitting that you can't *have* it all, you need to admit you can't *do* it all. Experiment with working in groups and asking for help whenever it's appropriate. Learn to think of these activities as sensible ways to manage your responsibilities, not signs of weakness or incompetence.

4. When planning your schedule, strike an appropriate balance between what you WANT to do personally and what you NEED to do to meet academic demands.

Your own personal wants are things that *you* consider important and would like to do, like watching the U.S. Open on TV. Academic demands, on the other hand, tend to be things that *others* consider important or that you feel you should get done, whether you like it or not, like completing your term paper. If you make this distinction in your mind whenever you're planning your day, it will help guarantee that you don't spend too much of your time on one kind of task and too little on the other.

This mental check will also help you develop a more positive attitude toward time. Rather than viewing it as a problem ("I'll never have enough time to do all this work"), you'll start seeing it as an ally ("I'm going to make time this weekend to get my paper done and watch the game").

Of course, the best situation is when an academic demand is also something you genuinely want to do—for instance, writing a term paper on a topic you really care about. In this situation, you come close to having it all!

5. Don't think about doing things to please others if it will be at the expense of your own academic success.

Nip in the bud any thoughts you have about taking on tasks or working hard just to gain someone else's approval.

Strive more toward satisfying your own goals! Learn to plan how you're going to spend your time and energy each day according to rules and schedules that make sense to you, instead of according to what other people want. It may temporarily feel good to win a friend's favor, but don't aim for this feeling if it's going to involve not taking proper care of your own school-related responsibilities.

As an overdoer procrastinator, you need to develop more self-respect and greater self-management skills by limiting the extent to which you're available to others. Tell yourself that you're not always going to go along with what others want you to do. If you do decide that you can and should help someone, make sure it fits into your schedule.

It's also important for you to avoid falling into the trap of feeling guilty or ashamed. Being down on yourself may lead to your being more inappropriately compliant toward others. It can be wonderful to help someone else out of love, compassion, or high regard. It can also be great to work hard for others out of sheer pleasure in the work. However, it can only be self-damaging to lend other people a hand just to win their approval, or to work excessively hard for others just to prove to yourself that you're a worthy person.

6. Think about how YOU are going to control things, instead of simply letting them happen or letting yourself be controlled.

To stop thinking like an overdoer procrastinator, you need to start envisioning yourself as the master of your life, rather than its victim. After all, most of the pressure and fatigue you experience while you're working so hard stems from the feeling that other people (especially teachers) and other events (especially school assignments) have you at their mercy. If you learn to regard yourself as the one who's most responsible for organizing your time and energy each day, you'll find that you're all the more motivated and competent to do so.

Guidelines for Speaking

1. Go ahead and say no to others when you feel it's appropriate.

If you can bring yourself to say no more often—especially when deep down you're thinking no—you'll find it much easier to stick to your priorities and get your most important work finished in a timely manner. As a bonus, you'll also develop more self-confidence and self-esteem. Always remember: The more you learn to say no when it's appropriate, the greater value your yes will ultimately have.

Bear in mind that there are many different types of no to choose from, including the blunt no, and the more polite and accommodating no, such as "no, thanks," "I'm sorry, no," "no, I'd like to, but I just don't have the time," "no, I can't today, but I can next week." Grant yourself the freedom to use whatever type of no best fits your mood and the situation.

2. Speak about your obligations as based on choices you have made, rather than on demands over which you have no control.

As an overdoer procrastinator, you need to guard against using conversations to gripe about things or to fish for sympathy. Instead, use them to help you make constructive decisions. This means talking about *the goals you want to accomplish,* and then inviting suggestions from others, rather than dwelling on *the work that's bothering you,* then waiting for others to pity or console you.

Let's suppose, for example, that you have an appointment with your advisor that you hate going to. If you want to talk about that appointment with a friend, don't just say, "I'm really dreading this appointment I have to go to" (burden-oriented). Instead, say something like, "I want my advisor to help me choose the courses I need for next semester, and I'm looking forward to getting that accomplished" (goal-oriented).

3. To strengthen your sense of controlling your own time, replace "I should" or "I'm supposed to" in your conversations with "I will" or "I want to."

Overdoer procrastinators typically speak in terms of what they *should* do or what they're *supposed to* do rather than what they *will* do or *want to* do. In doing so, they reinforce their sense of passiveness. Listen to what you say in your conversations, and change this pattern, so that you'll think of yourself and your situations in more positive, active ways. For example, rather than saying, "I'm *supposed to* go to the library to do research for my term paper," say, "I *will* go to the library to do research for my term paper."

4. To reinforce the fact that you're entitled to relax, talk more openly and less defensively about times when you don't work hard.

As an overdoer procrastinator, you're inclined to feel guilty or ashamed about not working. You wind up saying things like, "I wasted the whole weekend and didn't get a thing done on my paper." Avoid making such self-punishing statements. Instead, learn to say more positive things about nonworking times, like, "I spent the weekend thinking about things I could do this summer" or "I relaxed this weekend and caught up on some music I've been wanting to listen to."

5. Avoid describing yourself in conversations as a powerless or overwhelmed student.

As much as possible, guard against saying things that depict you as a victim, like, "I've got so much reading to do I don't know where to begin," "I have no choice," "this pace is killing me," or "there's nothing I can do about it." Remember: What you say plays a big role in determining your own self-image and the image others have of you. The more you can characterize yourself as a competent person capable of controlling your own life, the easier it will be to evolve into just that kind of person!

Guidelines for Acting

1. Strive to become more PROACTIVE (for example, figuring out how you'd like to do an assignment) and less REACTIVE (doing only what you think the teacher expects).

Like their defier counterparts, overdoer procrastinators tend to focus their attention too strongly on what others are demanding of them. The defier's impulse is to reject others' demands, while the overdoer's impulse is to take them on. Like the defier, you need to train yourself to give importance to what *you* want to do—the activities that best serve your personal goals—in addition to what *others* want you to do.

Of course, you may have to do certain school assignments as given, but do so in the spirit of meeting your own academic goals, rather than only satisfying the instructor or professor. You also need to be responsive to a certain degree to the needs of your friends and loved ones. But remember that there's a big difference between being appropriately *responsive* and being automatically *reactive*. Appreciate that you usually have more choices in life than you realize.

2. Develop a habit of reviewing your plans each day to determine the best ways of getting things done.

Early in the morning (or even the night before), look over all the tasks that you want or need to get done in the day to come. Then ask yourself these three basic questions:

• Which tasks are relatively unimportant and can be *eliminated?*

• Which ones can be *shared* with, or *delegated* to, someone else?

• Which tasks can be *consolidated*—that is, done at the same time or back-to-back?

You will be amazed at how much more time is suddenly available to you, once you've decided to eliminate, delegate, and consolidate.

3. Be sure to incorporate social and personal activities into your daily schedule that recharge your energy and interest in student life.

As a student, your days can become so filled with academic responsibilities, chores, and simple camaraderie that you neglect your responsibilities to yourself as a vital human being. Keep your mind, body, and spirit in good shape by regularly doing things that give you a personal sense of well-being. Occasionally it may mean doing something short and simple, like taking a walk, calling a friend, or playing the piano. Other times, it might involve doing something more ambitious, like spending a weekend in the wilderness, writing a short story, or having a heavy-duty workout at the gym.

Once you've scheduled such activities, don't skip them because you assume they're expendable! The more regularly and responsibly you engage in them, the more you'll realize that they greatly enhance your overall productivity.

4. To learn that you don't have to do everything yourself, ask for help whenever appropriate.

As a person who wants to be self-reliant, you're naturally hesitant to do this, but therein lies one of your greatest handicaps. You can learn a lot from other people who tend to manage their workloads more effectively. If you're in a jam, see if they're interested in giving you a hand, and then watch what they do!

You need to realize that everyone needs help from time to time, whether they ask for it or not. It's not going to make people think less of you if you turn to them with a problem or crisis. It's just as likely to make them think more highly of you for valuing their assistance. And if the people you ask say no, it doesn't mean they're rejecting you. It just means they're saying "no" to helping out on the task—at least at this time. Usually they have a perfectly good reason of their own that has nothing to do with you.

5. Form study groups or engage in group projects that can help you learn to work more effectively.

Overdoer procrastinators find it difficult not only to pace their own time and energy well, but also to cooperate more productively with others. You can help yourself overcome both kinds of difficulties by engaging in more group efforts to get tasks completed.

In a group context, you can observe the more constructive work habits of people who are not overdoers or procrastinators. You can also discover how to go about doing your own fair share of the work, rather than taking on more than you can handle. The experience will help you both in college and in the world beyond college, where many projects involve working with others as collaborators and partners—each person doing his or her own part of the job.

8

Making the Change

If you have read this far, you are no doubt aware of how much procrastination has cost you academically. Hopefully you are also motivated to do something about it. Yet changing ingrained patterns isn't easy. It requires managing your time and energy in many ways that are new to you. These ways don't come automatically or comfortably at first. Many of them you have already read about. Others you will only discover and learn to apply as you keep moving steadily forward.

Changing a lifelong habit is a continuing process of making yourself more and more aware of what you do, how you feel, and what you want to accomplish. There are three stages in this process, and passing successfully from stage to stage takes not only your time and energy, but also your sincere and lasting determination:

1. *The "On Your Mark" Stage:* from denial to awareness

2. *The "Get Set" Stage:* from awareness to commitment

3. *The "GO!" Stage:* from commitment to making it happen

Let's examine each of these stages individually.

The Three Stages of Change

1. The "On Your Mark" Stage: from denial to awareness

Denial is actually a *pre*-change or *anti*-change condition, in which a person doesn't even acknowledge that he or she has a problem. For some people, this blindness is a deliberate means of avoiding responsibility. For others, it involves a genuine lack of self-awareness. Either way, people in denial are focused on what's *outside* of them, instead of what's *inside*.

When you're caught in denial, you may know you have a procrastination problem but project the blame for it elsewhere. If other people criticize *you,* you may defensively view *them* as the problem: They don't understand, they're being unfair, they're bugging you! You may sometimes feel like changing your ways, but it's just a passing urge in response to some outside pressure, such as low grades, concerned teachers, disappointed parents, or the threat of losing a job.

To get beyond your denial, you need to increase your self-awareness so that you see your life more in terms of what *you* do, who *you* are, and what *you* want. Only then will you be motivated enough to make a real change.

2. The "Get Set" Stage: from awareness to commitment

Once you accept responsibility for your procrastination problem, you may still resist changing your ways. You may assume that you can just learn to live with the problem without getting so upset about it. You may think that simple awareness of the problem will eventually cause it to go away on its own. Or you may secretly hope that something magical will come along to banish the problem: an unexpected surge of fresh resolve, an inspirational teacher, a financial windfall, a new love.

Meanwhile, you keep relying heavily on BUT factors to explain your lack of initiative: Yes, I'd like to change, BUT I'm too lazy, BUT it's too difficult, BUT I'm too busy, BUT I can't, and so on. This rationalizing helps you save face, but it also reinforces your problems and often makes them even worse.

You may also say, "One part of me wants to change, BUT the other part doesn't." This thinking suggests that there are several selves inside of you that can't possibly make peace with each other, such as a child self ("I want to play") at odds with an adult self ("I need to meet my goals"), or a superhero self ("I want to accomplish stupendous feats") in conflict with a slug self ("I want to lie around and do nothing").

In fact, these inner selves can be reconciled with each other if you develop control of your time and energy, and give each self its proper share. You can, for example, enable your adult self to complete its mission so efficiently that your child self has ample opportunity to satisfy its needs as well. Or you can grant permission to your sluglike self to watch football games all weekend, if you allow your superhero self to reign supreme the week before.

You also need to guard against wasting your time and energy regretting the past instead of moving forward toward doing better *this* semester or quarter. Here are some guidelines for using regrets to motivate change instead of stonewalling it:

• *Let your regrets be self-educational.* Regrets can serve a good purpose by calling your attention to what is truly most important to you. If, for example, you often regret not having outlined your papers more thoroughly before starting to write them, you have strong evidence that you need to do better outlining in the future.

• *Use regrets as rallying cries for change.* Don't simply resort to regretting as a means of complaining or beating yourself over the head. Make it a basis for thinking, saying, or doing things that are more positive in nature. The mottos "I deserve better!" or "I'll show everybody!" or "This time will be different!" can be great self-energizers.

• *Anticipate future regrets before you make decisions.* Before acting on impulse, give serious thought to what the consequences could be, and what you could reasonably do to minimize risks. This strategy helps you protect yourself from having regrets later. For example, if you want to skip class, try contacting someone in advance who'd be willing to lend you his or her notes afterwards (advance notice might help to ensure that the notes are good or at least legible).

Aside from regret, another emotion that can keep students too paralyzed to change is *guilt*. Like nursing regrets, wallowing in guilt is a way of admitting the need for change without doing anything about it. Those who recognize their obligation—and capacity—to move beyond guilt toward positive change receive a wonderful reward: Their guilt dissipates!

3 The "GO!" Stage: from commitment to making it happen

Now you're ready! You know that it doesn't make sense to waste your time saying you want to change, but then doing nothing about it. In your moments of truth, you realize how much you've disappointed yourself by allowing procrastination to keep you from accomplishing the things you really wanted to do. You'll need to work hard to make the changes recommended in this book, but now you're prepared to experience firsthand the personal power you can gain through the magic of *thinking decisively, speaking decisively,* and *acting decisively.*

• *Thinking decisively.* Everything begins with the mind: Change your attitude, and you're well on your way toward transforming your life. Above all, practice the guidelines for Changing How You Think that apply to your most significant procrastination styles, according to the quizzes you took earlier in this book. With a little effort and perseverance, these new ways of thinking will soon become second nature to you. When they do, you'll think much more creatively, optimistically, and self-confidently about yourself and your future.

• *Speaking decisively.* Your choice of words greatly influences how you look at yourself, your life, and the tasks that lie before you. Because speech affects thought, and thought affects action, your words not only *describe* situations, but also help *determine* them. When you express yourself you are influencing your own thoughts, whether or not you're aware of doing so. With this in mind, choose more active and confident words, so that you put yourself in the best possible position to accomplish your goals.

Also, because procrastinators are invariably "yes, BUT" people, it is crucial for you to monitor those statements then transform them into more constructive statements as follows:

• *Change your placement of BUT.* The significant part of a BUT statement is always what comes *after* the BUT. What comes before is only the qualifier. Therefore, instead of saying, for example, "I'd like to be more focused on my studies, BUT I'm easily distracted," put the negative part *first,* and the positive part *last,* so that you end on an upbeat note—"I'm easily distracted, BUT I'd like to be more focused on my studies."

• *Turn your BUT statements into AND statements.* Rather than saying, for example, "I'd like to be more focused on my studies, BUT I'm easily distracted," say, "I'd like to be more focused on my studies AND I'm easily distracted." In shifting from BUT to AND, you acknowledge that you have *two* choices in front of you: The negative one doesn't simply cancel out the positive one. You can then go on to figure out how you're going to resolve the conflict with a SO statement: "I'd like to be more focused on my studies, AND I'm easily distracted, SO I'm going to do as much studying as possible in the library, which isn't so noisy."

• *Acting decisively.* Acting decisively is easier said than done. Every type of procrastinator experiences some trouble following up their motivating words with actual deeds. However, two types find it especially difficult: dreamers, who easily substitute fantasizing for doing, and passive-aggressive defiers, who have an entrenched habit of saying one thing and doing another. To ensure that you act as decisively as you speak, faithfully follow the Guidelines for Acting that apply to your major procrastination styles.

In addition, become more consciously aware of the personal reasons why you say you'll do something, and then don't do it. For example, do you speak before you've given sufficient thought to what's realistic for you to do? Do you wind up doubting yourself too much to live up to your word? If you conscientiously strive to overcome these self-defeating patterns, you'll be surprised how soon your words and your deeds join together to enable you to be a more integrated, take-charge person!

Motivating Yourself to Change

Change comes about by having the vision for yourself, believing in yourself, working to get something that you *say is important.*

—OPRAH WINFREY

The key to strong and lasting personal transformation lies in encouraging yourself to *want* to change. When change is something you genuinely desire, you'll move toward it as naturally as a flower turns toward sunlight. Ordering, threatening, or punishing yourself to change is not the answer. It may get you started—or restarted—when you're stalled along the road, but it won't get you all the way to your goal.

You have to know in your heart what you truly want for yourself or you'll find it too easy to give up at the first hint of frustration. In the final analysis, it's all up to you: how deeply you care about what you say is important to you, and how earnestly you strive to achieve it. As Thomas Edison said, "Genius is one percent inspiration, and ninety-nine percent perspiration."

This book has provided you with a lot of useful information. Now *you* need to provide the motivation. You can inspire yourself to change by doing the following things:

• **Keep in mind specific reasons why it's good for you to change.**

In addition to reminding yourself of the harmful consequences you experienced when you procrastinated, be sure to recall the triumphant times you had when when you did *not* procrastinate. Other items to remember are:

- • personal dreams or goals that depend upon your changing

- • positive images of yourself (perhaps from the past, perhaps imaginary) that you want to actualize

- • personal heroes (real or mythical) that you'd like to emulate

Compose a list of these reasons and keep it handy, so that you have something specific to look at when you need more motivation.

• **Play a game called "Avoid Avoiding."**

Procrastination is essentially an unresolved approach-avoidance conflict: You want or need to do the task (approach), BUT you don't (avoidance). The "Avoid Avoiding" game is an adventurous way of challenging yourself to enact the *approach* part of the conflict despite your contrary pull toward *avoidance*.

Let's imagine, for instance, that you're tempted to procrastinate because of the following BUT factor: "I'd like to spend more time studying each night, BUT I've got too many other things to do." Instead of just giving up in the face of this conflict, or constantly getting nowhere by making one step forward followed by one step backward, invite yourself to play Avoid Avoiding. First, acknowledge that you *do* have this feeling that there are "too many other things to do." Then, go ahead and, despite the feeling, study a half hour longer each night.

As a result of this decision, you're sure to find ways that you can live with the extra half hour of studying. This discovery will help temper any future inclination to say—and, therefore, believe—so automatically that you can't do something because you have too many other things to do.

• Make the most out of any criticism you receive.

Criticism from an instructor, professor, or friend will only wound you, *if* you let it. When you're in the process of changing, you're bound to be unusually sensitive to the reactions of others, so it's vital to remember that you have three options whenever you're criticized:

• You can ignore the criticism altogether;

• You can let the criticism hurt you so much that you either go into your shell or attack the critic; or

• You can review the criticism to see if it has anything to teach you.

The latter choice—by far the most potentially helpful—means considering criticism as a learning tool. Whenever someone else says something critical to you, consider their words as nondefensively as you can. Tell yourself that even if it hurts, you can learn a lot from other people about your own weaknesses or faults. Then, if you do recognize some value in what they've revealed to you, take it upon yourself to work with what you've learned.

For example, suppose you get a lower-than-expected grade on a research paper, and your teacher tears apart your premise, your methodology, and your results. It's bound to hurt, so allow yourself to feel that hurt instead of denying it. Then, as soon as you're able, say to yourself, "Okay, what can I learn from this?" Among other things, you might learn the following:

- Get preapproval from the professor on your premise and methodology before going any further with a paper.

- Figure out how to express certain kinds of thoughts more clearly on paper, so that your language is less likely to cause misunderstanding or confusion.

- Be wary of relying on the same kinds of source materials in the future.

Using criticism constructively, whether or not others offer it in that spirit, is usually the way professional athletes treat criticism of their performance from judges or coaches. They listen and utilize what they think is useful to help them improve their physical skills, psychological stamina, emotional resilience, and overall presentation.

• When you falter, get back on track.

In making a major life change like overcoming chronic procrastination, the most crucial factor is not really *how well* or
how quickly you move toward doing things more effectively, but *that* you move in the right direction. You may occasionally, or even consistently, take small steps instead of
big ones. You may also find yourself periodically stuck for a
while, or taking a backwards-moving detour from the main
path. No matter what your style is, just be sure to move *as
much* and *as often as you can* in a forward direction.

As you progress, you will inevitably experience a disturbing
lapse into your old, self-defeating habits of postponing or
dawdling on tasks that are important. It may come as part of
a general slump in your life, when it's difficult to do anything
constructive, or it may be a response to an especially challenging situation that upsets your schedule and your equilibrium.

Whatever the cause of the problem, the solution for
keeping the change process alive is learning to view the setback as a temporary one. Rather than feeling guilty about
it, which undermines your ability to bounce back, regard it
as the perfect occasion to revitalize your commitment and
prove to yourself that you can do it!

The process of change can take months or maybe even
years, as you go about practicing, assimilating, and reinforcing more decisive, change-related thoughts, speaking
patterns, and behaviors. The wonder and beauty of the
process is that it keeps on getting easier and more satisfying
the more you apply yourself to it.

• Reward yourself for progress.

It's good to pat yourself on the back when you've followed
a guideline, achieved a milestone, or received a genuine

compliment in your process of change. It's even better, however, to give yourself a specific reward. Doing so enables you to *experience* your triumph more fully, and, as a result, gain more vivid sense memories to associate with being successful.

An excellent way to establish an ongoing reward system is to develop the general habit of working *before* you play. Procrastinators too often do the opposite, and either never get around to the working phase or start it far too late.

The secret to using the "work first" approach successfully is not to get too fanatical about it, or you may overlook a genuine need for self-revitalizing play. Learn to distinguish between play activities that can truly benefit you by lifting your spirits and ones that are primarily attractive as ways to dodge responsibilities.

A more specific reward system is to promise yourself a particular treat for doing something in a timely and effective manner. Here are some ideas:

• Maintain an ongoing "reward list" of things that you like to buy for yourself. Then, identify one item from this list *before* doing a task as a reward that you'll give yourself for a job well done. This prior determination makes the item much more valuable as an incentive while you're actually doing the task. Your list may include CDs, clothes, sporting gear, or tickets to a game or show.

• Plan to treat yourself to a special meal or movie. If it's a meal, it could involve trying out a new restaurant, visiting an old favorite, or taking your best-loved foods on a picnic in the park. If it's a movie, it could mean going out to see a first-run movie, or renting one that you have long wanted to see. Do it just for yourself, or invite someone you like to join you. If you do share the experience, be sure to tell the other person why it's happening! Talking about your sense of accomplishment will help reinforce it.

• Do something that you'll enjoy physically, such as playing your favorite sport, treating yourself to a full body massage, or taking a walk along the shore. You'll be making an important association between feeling good physically and feeling good about yourself that will help move the change process along.

Living Free from Procrastination

Many students who come to me for help tell me that they're ambivalent about change because they fear the solution to procrastination will involve much harder work than they've ever done before, with much less fun to compensate.

Nothing could be further from the truth! Former clients who have successfully beat their procrastination problems report just the opposite experience: They're able to meet their responsibilities with greater personal comfort and satisfaction, and they get far more enjoyment out of their lives. Much to their surprise, they discover that liberating themselves from their self-crippling habits means not only putting more into their life, but getting more out of it!

The life of a student who's no longer a procrastinator actually becomes easier, rather than harder. The secret to making this positive transformation in your own life lies in overcoming whatever natural resistance you have to change. The words expressed by the Roman orator Terence in 150 B.C. are just as true now: "There is nothing so easy but it becomes difficult when you do it reluctantly."

Here's what today's ex-procrastinators have to say about living free from procrastination:

• *They feel happier and prouder about who they are.* Before overcoming their procrastination habits, they didn't feel very good about themselves. They doubted their sincerity as planners and their ability as doers. Their resulting guilt and shame kept them from taking much pleasure in what they did manage to accomplish, or even in themselves as individuals.

Changing their procrastinating ways helped them gain personal strength, self-confidence, and self-respect. Now the life they lead without procrastination keeps on fueling that better, more optimistic sense of self. They've freed themselves from their former fears of failing, of making mistakes, of saying no to inappropriate demands, of being bored, of taking risks.

Jon, the former perfectionist procrastinator featured in chapter 2, said, "It's so much more fun to be a human being than to be a perfectionist with impossible goals. I finally realized that the lofty ambitions I once set for myself were not realistic, and I didn't need to achieve them to have a good life. I somehow just thought I had to be better than everyone else to be successful. It wasn't true! The unrealistic expectations were all in my head, and all they were doing was making my life one big headache!"

Jerry, the former crisis-maker procrastinator we met in chapter 5, declared, "I learned that I can get much more pleasure out of doing things at the right time than waiting for the emergency signal. I finally said to myself: I want to do things now, when I have the time to do them, rather then later on, when I know it will be so much more stressful. I don't want to live constantly in chaos when I really don't have to!"

• *They feel better about doing things that need to be done*. As procrastinators, they either dreaded, resented, or denied many of their responsibilities. To them, any and every task was a heavy problem to face, with yet another high possibility of failure attached, given their strong tendency to avoid work or put it off.

Now that they've changed their procrastinating ways, their responsibilities seem lighter, and less burdensome. They get more pleasure out of meeting them as they get increasingly better at doing so.

Holly, the former overdoer procrastinator in chapter 7, told me, "I've discovered that I like doing many of the assignments that are important for me to do. It's so much more gratifying than my old pattern, which was trying to get other people to like me by always doing what they wanted. Now that I'm putting more time into meeting my own objectives, I respect myself a lot more!"

• *They get more respect from others*. As chronic procrastinators, they complicated not only their own lives, but also the lives of the people around them. Time and again they seduced their friends, lovers, family members, and teachers into playing along with their tedious waiting games. Eventually these other people were compelled to assume the thankless roles of taskmasters, naggers, critics, or executioners. It's no wonder that procrastinators so often alienate the people they most care about, and come to regard them as antagonists instead of allies!

When individuals break through their procrastinating habits, they're free to relate to others more authentically, positively, and confidentially. As they do so, they develop relationships that are more solidly and enjoyably based on mutual respect.

Shelley, the former defier procrastinator profiled in

chapter 6, remarked, "I always felt that someone else had to make me work, that I wasn't going to do it on my own. Now that I take it upon myself to get things done, I find that I actually enjoy doing a lot of the work! Even more, I like that others value me for what I'm doing for myself. It's so much nicer to earn people's respect than to be fighting them all the time."

• *They feel more mastery over their use of time.* As procrastinators, they frequently couldn't concentrate on their work, were easily lured away from it, and constantly viewed themselves as victims rather than masters of time. As ex-procrastinators, they have a greater sense of power over their lives. They focus more effectively on the tasks they most need to do and finish them according to schedules that they themselves create.

Melissa, the former worrier procrastinator in chapter 4, revealed, "The single most helpful thing I learned was not to get so worked up over the great, big, overwhelming chore in front me. Right away I break apart that chore into a bunch of smaller, better-looking ones that are much more my size. Then, one by one, I get those little chores done until the only thing left in front of me is one more little chore, and it's all over. I feel as if I've taught myself a secret—how to master anything."

• *They live a life that's smoother, well-balanced, and more personally meaningful.* Before freeing themselves from procrastination, they lived constantly on the brink of disaster, never really certain they could accomplish what they needed or wanted to do. They had to face the fact that they probably wouldn't accomplish *anything* without having to go through a great deal of pressure, frustration, and pain. Life was always a gamble for mere survival: Perhaps things would turn out okay, perhaps they wouldn't. It was an existence fraught with chaos and insecurity.

Free from procrastination, they live in greater harmony with the natural rhythms of their own life and the world around them. They feel in control of their fate, instead of at the mercy of blind chance. They have faith in themselves, their goals, and their newly developed decision-making and task-managing skills. They are moving toward a future that's more clearly self-defined, instead of being tossed about in a tempest of confusion and uncertainty.

Kathi, the former dreamer procrastinator featured in chapter 3, told me, "I used to prefer living in fantasyland rather than dealing with the real world. Now I know that the Earth is a pretty neat place to be. It's where I belong. I don't feel so empty, or phony, or lonely anymore. I feel much closer to my studies, to my friends and family, and to myself."

Time is a limited, precious, perishable asset. Once it's gone, it can never be replaced. Years from now, if you look back over your academic years and believe that procrastination stole precious time from you, preventing you from achieving your goals, or even keeping you from setting any goals, you will surely feel cheated and bemoan the fact that you wasted such a vital resource.

Instead, wouldn't it be great if you felt that you used your time well to accomplish many important goals, to develop lots of rewarding relationships, and to participate in a wide variety of meaningful experiences? Beating procrastination will reward you with all that and more!

I'm confident that this book has been a real eye-opener for you. I know that if you take it to heart, it will do wonders for you, providing you with a better feeling about yourself, your student experience, and your preparation for the future.

Time will tell!

5   5/01

1/03 10   3/03

2/04   14   7/03
8/05   (15)   5/05
4/10   (20)   2/10

3/12 (35)
3/19 (54) 1/19